Oh Twaddi!

CITIZEN *Khan's* GUIDE TO BRITAIN

CITIZEN *Khan* KI VILAYAT KI GUIDE

↖

(This is Urdu. Don't worry, rest of book all in English)

sphere

SPHERE

Copyright © 2016 by Adil Ray

Written by Adil Ray

Additional writing by
Anil Gupta, Richard Pinto, David Isaac, Waqas Saeed, Mahinder Bhogal

Design by Carrdesignstudio.com and Charlotte Stroomer

1 3 5 7 9 10 8 6 4 2

This paperback edition published in 2016 by Sphere

The moral right of the author has been asserted.

A CIP catalogue record for this book
is available from the British Library.

Printed in Germany

ISBN 978-0-7515-6711-3

Sphere
An imprint of
Little, Brown Book Group
Carmelite House
50 Victoria Embankment
London EC4Y 0DZ

An Hachette UK Company
www.hachette.co.uk

www.littlebrown.co.uk

**To all those who bought
this book.**

(If you are reading this in the shop,
now your fingerprints are on it you need
to get to the till immediately. Thank you.)

Contents

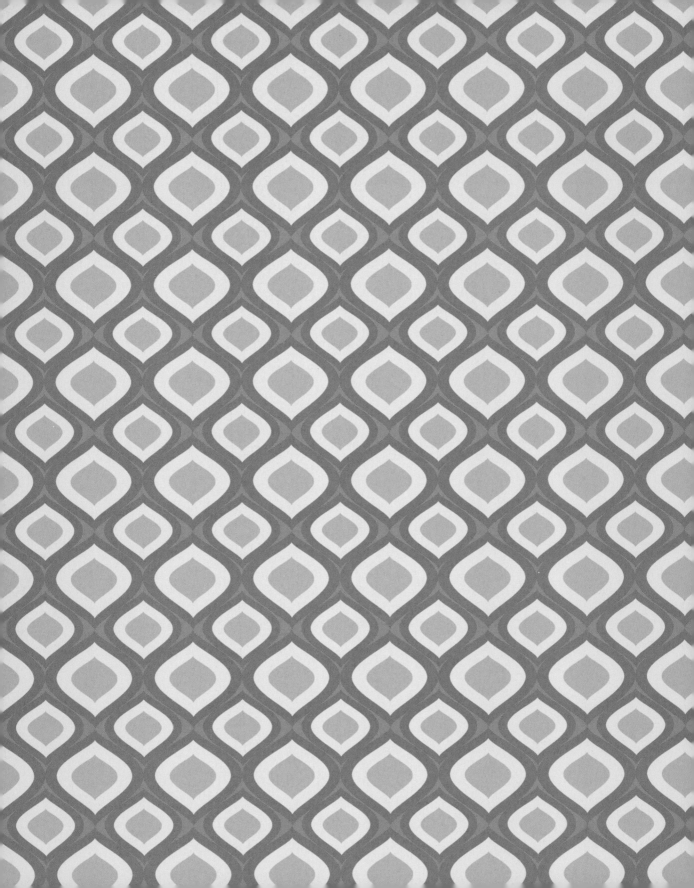

The Early Years

Asalaam Alaikum.

Oh Twaddi! Hello, Mr Khan speaking. K, H for Hat, A for Asian, N for Knowledge. Well, it's a great honour for me to have a book out, isn't it? After all, you must feel very honoured to be reading it. This book is very important. I hope it achieves exactly what it is intended to do – pay for my new bloomin' bathroom! I'm hoping to get one with gold taps and one of those showers with lots of squirty bits! Ooh yes!!

So where is best place for me to start? Well, how about the most important day in the world? No, not the Boxing Day sale at Next (that's a close second), I'm talking about the day I was born. Mr Khan Day. I was born on ~~an day of burth~~* in a street near Rawalpindi, Pakistan. I mean in an actual street. Well, when I say street, more of a gulley. People in the area pay tribute to me when they walk past the spot, you know like those blue plaque things you see on the side of a house for some boring inventor who once lived there. People travel far and wide to visit my birthplace.

*Dear editor please do not publish my date of birth as immigration and people from HMRC might be reading

My birthplace

That's my mother, Bibi, on the right. Look at her! So beautiful. My father used to call her Casio, after the classic watch, because 'she never stopped working'. You might be wondering where my father is in this photo. Well, when my mother was pregnant he went on holiday for 9 months. He believed that he had already fulfilled his part of the deal some months ago. Fair enough. And, he said, when my mum gave birth to my sister the year before, he had not seen that much water breaking since the Mangla Dam gave way back in 1962. He never quite recovered. For many years to come he would hide in his room during the monsoon. It brought back too many memories.

My mother

Rawalpindi's version of ASDA

So since he was out of town it was down to my mother to do all the shopping. So out she popped, and out I popped! She was on her way back from Pakistani version of Asda (which was basically just like British Asda – there's never any parking spaces, it's full of Pakistani staff and they have a very good halal section).

My mother was walking around a corner when suddenly there was an almighty bang. It was horrible. People were screaming, goats were climbing the trees and fruit carts were collapsing all over the place, all because the local butcher had just shot himself. Why? Because Hanif Mohammad had been given out LBW in the first test in Barbados. The sad thing is that if we had had DRS back then (that technology thingy that umpires use) he would still be alive today. Anyway the loud bang scared my mother and brought on her contraction thingies and as soon as the umpire put his finger up, out I came. So Mr Khan was born. And how lucky you people are . . .

World Events Timeline

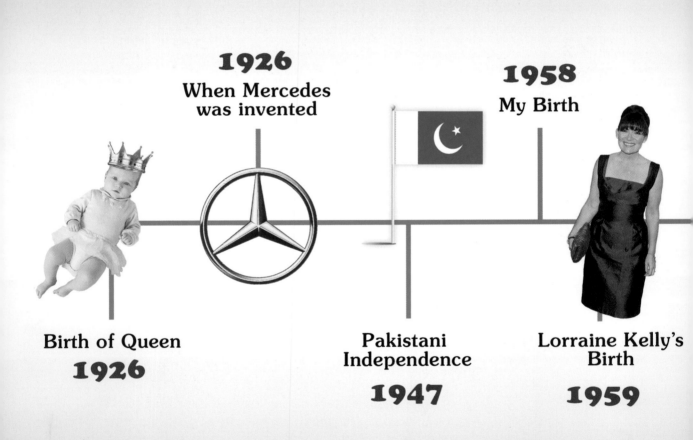

1926
When Mercedes
was invented

1958
My Birth

Birth of Queen
1926

Pakistani
Independence
1947

Lorraine Kelly's
Birth
1959

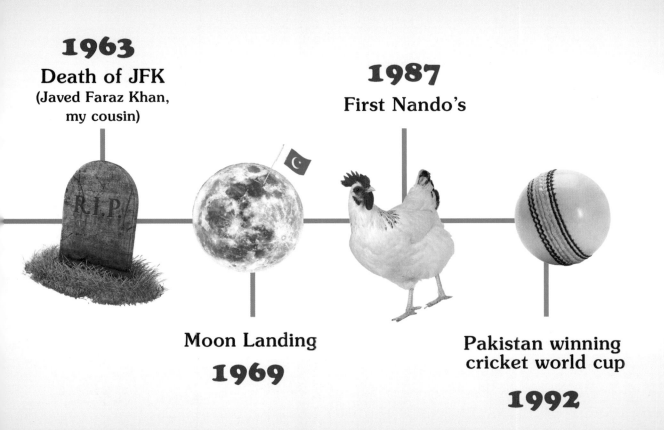

1963
Death of JFK
(Javed Faraz Khan,
my cousin)

1987
First Nando's

Moon Landing
1969

Pakistan winning
cricket world cup

1992

The Early Years: Work experience

Growing up as a child in Pakistan is a lot different to the UK.
Unless you are born in Birmingham or Bradford – then it's exactly the same.

The main thing about growing up as a child in Pakistan is that things just happen sooner. You leave school sooner, get a job sooner, get married sooner and in the end you die sooner, as life expectancy isn't very high. So I guess it makes sense to make the most of it.

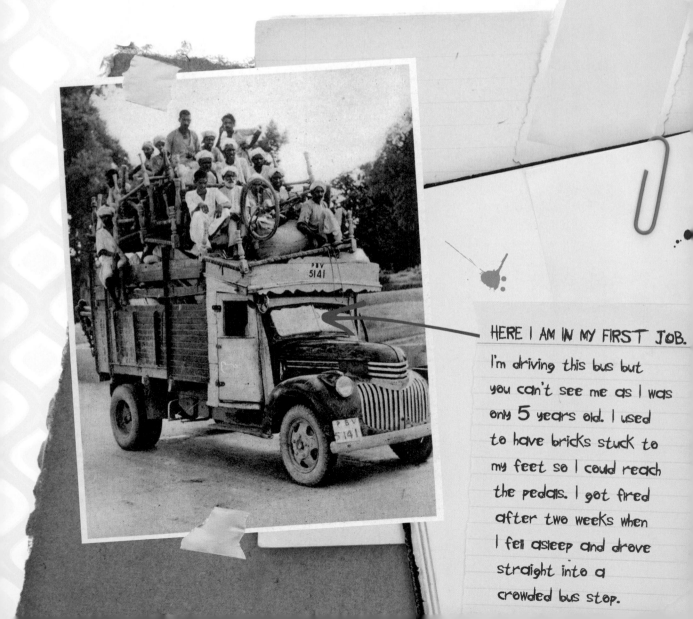

HERE I AM IN MY FIRST JOB.
I'm driving this bus but you can't see me as I was only 5 years old. I used to have bricks stuck to my feet so I could reach the pedals. I got fired after two weeks when I fell asleep and drove straight into a crowded bus stop.

HERE I AM AGED 7 IN MY
SECOND JOB.
I had a proper title and everything.
I was the Toilet Cleaner.

HERE I AM WORKING AS A
BUILDER.
The working conditions
weren't too bad. I only used
to work 14 hours in a day.
Then 10 hours at night.
Oh Twaddi!

32

But course we would do other things. Like chase birds. Yes, of course. Didn't all boys do that? Here's me and my cousins preparing the evening's dinner.

Sometimes we would go swimming at the local lido.

Swimming in the lake was always fun but also a challenge. There was one basic rule. The left side of the lake was for actual swimming and the right side for any releasing of bodily fluids. This wasn't always adhered to. I once got a mouthful of Abrar's you know what whilst attempting the front crawl.

But I know what you are thinking. What about girls? Did you ever talk to females, I hear you say? Of course we did! Here's my friend Saleem talking to one.

Oh, you mean actual girls. Yes. Look. There you are. This is my friend Iqbal with a girl. He used to talk to her lots. They had so much in common. Family for a start – they are cousins. They have been married now 35 years.

People often say to me, life in Pakistan must have been boring — not at all. Just like Birmingham's Broad Street on a Friday night and London's Pickleydically on a Saturday we boys knew how to have a great time. Here are some of the boys having drinks on a crazy Friday night in Rawalpindi.

Friday night Pindi!

Friday night in UK!

Can you spot the difference?

Let me tell you. In Pakistani photo they only drinking water so the round is free!

What do you mean they look miserable? That's bloomin' happy hour!

My neighbourhood

Most important thing: prayer mat

Air conditioning

Village bus: would not depart un 48 passengers on boa

A dog. Or as white people call it, a burglar alarm

Modern toilet

22

As you may know Pakistan was part of India (the best part) up until **1947.** Partition was a very tough time for all concerned and deciding how things got divided up was very tricky. Luckily I have managed to get my hands on the document that showed how things did get divided:

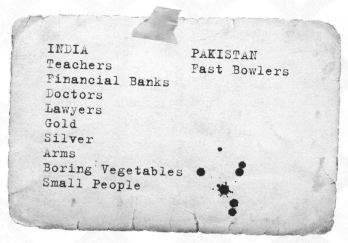

```
INDIA                    PAKISTAN
Teachers                 Fast Bowlers
Financial Banks
Doctors
Lawyers
Gold
Silver
Arms
Boring Vegetables
Small People
```

Of course, you can see we got the better deal, right?

Being part of India did mean of course we were under the British Empire. Some of the things the British introduced were beating us with sticks, turning us into servants, and the railways. Here's a few of us trying to escape Lahore when we heard that the British were coming with their rifles.

Back in Pakistan we kept up to date with British culture and events. This is my favourite photo of a few of the boys getting caught up in the excitement after England won the 1966 World Cup Final.

We even had a song that we used to sing:

ENG-UR-LUND, ENG-UR-LUND, ENG-UR-LUND
KICK YOUR BALLS, KICK YOUR BALLS, KICK YOUR BALLS,
WE SAVING UP FOR TICKET
TO SHOW YOU HOW TO PLAY CRICKET

It was very catchy, like a lot of things in Pakistan. Cholera, Typhoid . . .

We also remember looking to Britain for some of your great inventions. Like these little trailer things you presumably used to drive around your staff/mother-in-laws.

What a great idea.

But of course we all remember the 1969 Concorde maiden flight. We Pakistanis loved Concorde. We had a lot in common with Concorde – we both end up in every city in the world and we both got big noses!

Uncanny?

Many famous British people came to Pakistan in the 1960s but nobody was quite bigger than The Beatles. Actually Benny Hill came close. Wherever he went women were waiting for him! Here they are waiting for him at arrivals at Karachi Airport.

But we all remember Beatlemania in the 1960s and when the Beatles first arrived at Lahore Airport. Now that was an amazing day – all four of them just there right in front of us on the tarmac.

27

But of course I also remember the band The Beatles. Yes, we loved them; we considered them Pakistani anyway.

Georji was pretty much Muslim with that beard.

Rangoo loved his sitar.

Mukka never stops working. How much more Pakistani can you get?

John Lentils loved his Asian food. Especially daal. In fact he loved Asians so much he ended up marrying one, isn't it? Yoko must have been a good cook.

They came to Pakistan and really found themselves – which wasn't hard being the only four white people in the country. We even had our own tribute band:

The Beastles

So it's not difficult to work out why many of us came to England. We were excited by it. Especially when we were told we would have a great time there. We saw lots of pictures of Britain in the Pakistani papers:

Peaceful Britain

British Summertime

We couldn't wait!

One of the ways I learned so much about Britain was from the letters I received from my cousin who had already moved there. Here they are.

Dear Khanny baby...

I hope you're cool man! Yeah baby. There's a reason they call it the swinging sixties man!. The whole place is rocking!

I'm In London chilling with all the cool cats and chicks. I've had a lot of weed, I'm having a blast. It gives me the gas!

I live at a flower power commune, a man like you would really dig it here this place is like a farm with free love!

You know I have always loved you man, You are so cool. You would be one of the beautiful people, just hanging out on Mary Jane, dropping acid and getting stoned.

I must go but was hoping that my favourite cousin could help me out with a little bread?

Your dear cousin,

Abdul

Dear cousin Abdul

So nice to hear from you. You say such nice things! Beautiful People? Me? Thank you cousin.

You ask if I am cool? No I am not. Its 40 degrees here and we can no longer afford to pay the children from next village to wave the fans next to our beds!

I do hope you are ok because you mentioned the place is rocking. It's rocking here too. We are still suffering tremors from last weeks earthquake. As for the swinging sixties. Yes I know what you mean. Swing bowling seems to be the way to go for many cricket teams. Did you see Gareth Sobers? Amazing.

I am a bit worried that you are hanging out with cats and chicks? Have you had your jabs? Your Uncle Masood caught a viral infection from the village cat last week.

Now about these blasts you are having. I remember your troubled stomach very well and would insist that you lay off weeds and similar foods if they give you the gas, I have many strong memories of your blasts. We all do.

What do you mean by flower power? This farm of yours sounds very advanced, we are still using the old generator. It lasts an hour a day. Did you say love is free? Well now you know I like a bargain. In Pakistan love is not free. Do you know how much Pakistani wedding costs these days! As for me digging it when I get there, yes I am a very good digger, you should see how the farm looks now because of my effort. What's the pay like?

Now listen to me cousin Abdul. This Mary Jane woman. You know that I am respectful and would do no such thing. No wonder you were stoned afterwards. I mean I think stoning is a bit harsh as a punishment. We abandoned it in Pakistan some years ago. I am surprised the British are still persevering with it.

By the way, did you injure yourself when you dropped the acid? I dropped acid car battery on my foot last month. That was painful. Get some tiger balm on it.

Now regards the bread. Of course I can help you with bread, do they not have bread in London? I will get mum to make it immediately, how much do you need? Is that all you need? Just bread? Really? Are you sure I can't send you anything else?

Your cousin,

Khan or Khanny Baby. I like that.

Dear Khanny baby,

King of kings, you misunderstand me. We call money bread over here and the reason for my letter is that I need £100 to get a new set of wheels so that I can start transporting Mary Jane.

I thought who else would help me with the £150 but you! You really are the most reliable friend and cousin to see your way to sending me £200, you are the greatest, out of sight man!

Anyway, I hope you can help me out with the £250, I will make sure it gets back to you soon.

Please send a cheque for £300 in name of Abdul Hussain.

Your cousin,

Abdul

Dear cousin Abdul,

Apologies for my late response.

Oh Twaddi! This £300 has been difficult to arrange but of course, for you, I have managed to get the £300. Three hundred pounds is such a lot of money. The cost of our house actually. It would pay for our food for a year. But it's fine isn't it? It's so fine. I mean it's absolutely totally fine. As we are family. You are in England and you will not forget us here.

I will not go into the details of how I managed to get the money, only to say that I have used my entire savings from working morning till night in the cotton fields. It's fine. It really is. Anytime.

To reach the full £300 that you need, I have also had to sell our grandfather's harvesting machine, instead he now has a rake. He's much fitter these days.

But listen to me for £300 you can get a whole car, not just the wheels and as happy as I am for you, do not let Mary Jane take advantage of you, let her catch the bus or train.

Please find enclosed a cheque for the £300.

Please send photos of the car and write back soon.

Your cousin,

Khanny Baby, Beautiful Person.

I never heard from him again.

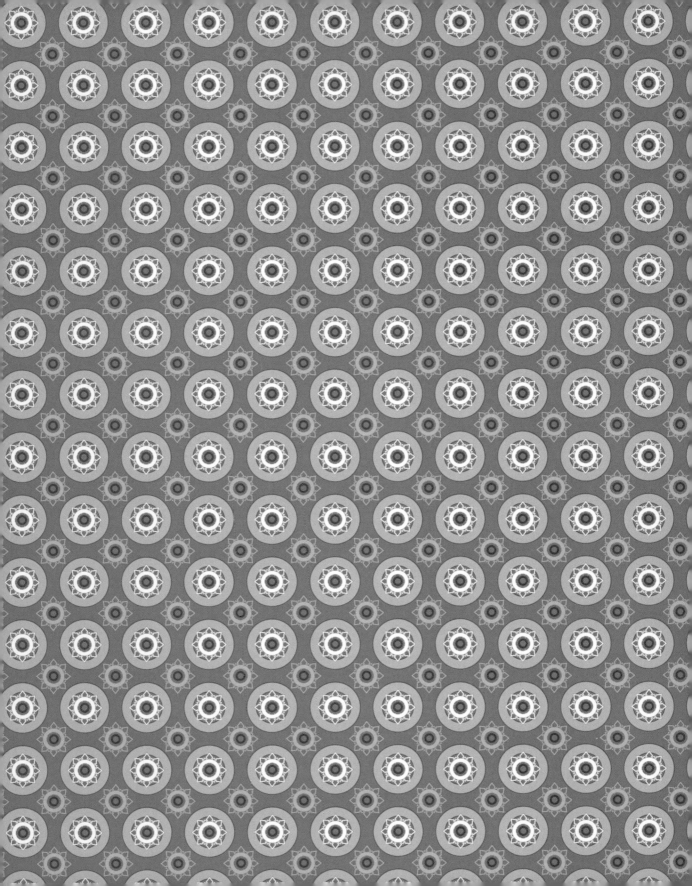

My Journey to the UK

Yes, this handsome fellow is yours truly, Mr Khan!

UNITED KINGDOM OF GREAT BRITAIN AND NORTHERN ISLAND

PASSPORT NUMBER

765345610

SURNAME-

KHAN

NATIONALITY-

PAKISTANI

SEX-

Sometimes

DOB -

PLACE OF BIRTH -

A street

OCCUPATION -

Yes please

<<GBRUK<<<SPECIMEN<<<KHAN<<<<MR<<<<<<<<<<<<<<<<<

Look, it's me, 1978.
Pakistani Travolta

37

So I was aged 21 and I decided I wanted to go to the UK. To get my money back from my thieving cousin, listen to more of Lentils and Mukka songs and watch some Benny Hill without being caught by my mother. But first I had to break the news to her. My mother was quite a tough lady. But it didn't stop me from trying my great powers of persuasion. This is how it went . . .

My mother was cooking in the outhouse. I peered in to make sure she didn't have a knife in her hand or any sharp and heavy objects in reaching distance. My mother never hesitated to throw things. Imagine a cross between Gordon Ramsay and Fatima Whitbread in Pakistani shalwar kameez. Exactly.

So I slowly approached like I was trying to grab a cricket ball from the side of a sleeping tiger. She turned. I think I broke wind immediately.

Me: Asalaam Alaikum, Mummy.

Mum: Walaikum Salaam. What do you want?

Me: It's a lovely day, isn't it?

Mum: It's 45 degrees and the chickens have crapped all over the veranda, so no.

Me: What's for dinner?

Mum: Your father hasn't brought any money home for 2 months now so we are eating bread and water.

Me: Oh yummy, my favourite. You hair looks nice, Mummy. Have you had it done?

Mum: What hair? Can't you see my hijab? You idiot.

Me: Oh yes. I meant the hair on ... your face. Looks nice.

Mum: Your dad has run out of razors.

Me: Well, this is lovely. Mum and son having a little chat. What could be better than this?

Mum: What would be better is if you cleaned that crap off the veranda.

Me: Ok, I will of course do that in a minute. But I just wanted to tell you something first.

Mum: What?

Me: Well ...

Mum: Yes?

Me: Well, I was thinking..

Mum: Yes?

Me: Can I use a brush to clean the chicken poop or do I have to use my feet again?

Mum: Feet. I need broom to whack your father in the goolies when he gets home. Anything else?

Me: I was thinking ...

Mum: Yes?

Me: I was thinking of moving to ...

Mum: Yes?

Me: I was thinking of moving to England.

MY MOTHER PUNCHES ME IN THE FACE, I FALL FLAT ON THE GROUND. THE END.

(Mum came with me in the ambulance. She needed a lift to the post office in town.)

Moving to the UK can be difficult. It's not easy – you need to have sheer dedication and determination – because the hardest thing for all immigrants is knowing what to pack.

1. Lots of thermal underwear

It's very important if coming to the UK that you bring along suitable clothing. Here is some thermal underwear – and this is just for the summer months.

2. Cricket Pads and Bat

Everybody knows that we Pakistanis have much better cricket equipment than the English. You should see our helmets. Always bring pads and a bat with you. Personally I didn't end up playing much cricket, but it came in very useful when we were being beaten up by the police in the Birmingham riots of 1985.

3. Rice

It's very difficult to know how much rice to bring. Exactly what is the legal allowance? Always try to bring in a few extra bags if you can.

4. A Goat

You can't have rice without meat – we are not Indian after all – so it is always worth bringing along a goat. If you are worried about smuggling a goat in try dressing it up in clothing and putting on some glasses. It might look like a hairy cousin.

Look, A mixed-race goat. Already integrating!

5. A Pakistani Blanket

Fellow Pakistanis will know about these 10-tonne blankets. They are very, very well-known and very, very heavy. In fact you need three other people to lift this blanket and place it on top of you when you go to sleep. But they do keep you warm for a long time. Do remember to ask someone to be there in the morning to take it off or you might end up like my Uncle Fawad.

One of the other challenges of coming to the UK is dealing with check-in at a Pakistani Airport. You get asked a lot of questions and there are lots of forms to fill in. Did you pack this bag yourself? Of course I didn't – my wife/sister did! I mean what kind of silly question is that? Idiots. It's like when you're in bloomin' doctor's surgery and someone comes in and says 'You alright?' It's always someone English, you know, a bit podgy and tattoos etc. Of course I am not bloomin' alright. If I was alright why would I be at the bloomin' doctor's? I tell you what, there's something wrong with people like that. At least they're at the bloomin' doctor's, so they can get checked out.

So where was I before I was so rudely interrupted by podgy man? Ah yes, when you're at check-in here's an example of the form you need to fill in.

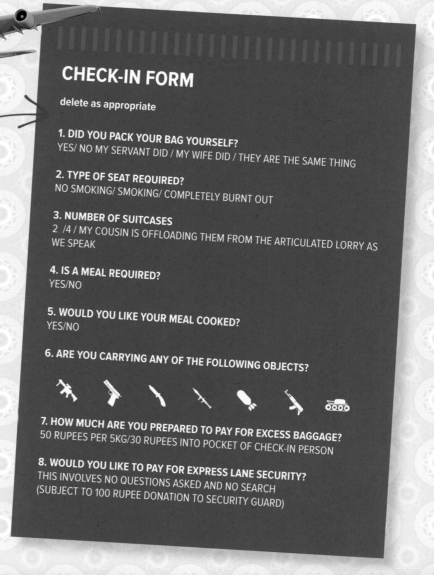

CHECK-IN FORM

delete as appropriate

1. DID YOU PACK YOUR BAG YOURSELF?
YES/ NO MY SERVANT DID / MY WIFE DID / THEY ARE THE SAME THING

2. TYPE OF SEAT REQUIRED?
NO SMOKING/ SMOKING/ COMPLETELY BURNT OUT

3. NUMBER OF SUITCASES
2 /4 / MY COUSIN IS OFFLOADING THEM FROM THE ARTICULATED LORRY AS WE SPEAK

4. IS A MEAL REQUIRED?
YES/NO

5. WOULD YOU LIKE YOUR MEAL COOKED?
YES/NO

6. ARE YOU CARRYING ANY OF THE FOLLOWING OBJECTS?

7. HOW MUCH ARE YOU PREPARED TO PAY FOR EXCESS BAGGAGE?
50 RUPEES PER 5KG/30 RUPEES INTO POCKET OF CHECK-IN PERSON

8. WOULD YOU LIKE TO PAY FOR EXPRESS LANE SECURITY?
THIS INVOLVES NO QUESTIONS ASKED AND NO SEARCH
(SUBJECT TO 100 RUPEE DONATION TO SECURITY GUARD)

Inflight Entertainment

• Pakistani in-flight entertainment is like no other, it's in a league of its own. The entertainment isn't just restricted to your seat-back TV. Here are a few things you can look forward to:

• If you are lucky you will come across an argument over someone staring at someone else's wife. This will often result in our very own **WWE: Hulk Hamid meets Abdul the Giant.** Enjoy your ringside seat.

• The **Pakistani Snoring Championships** are a regular occurrence mid-flight. The loudest snore ever recorded was by a Mrs Mahroof of Jhelum. She was so loud she woke up the pilot!

• On one trip to the UK my goat, Bilal, was in the lead of the **goat-races** after completing twenty-six laps around the economy cabin, but eventually tired and veered off into first class before being shot by one the fellow passengers. They served goat curry that flight.

We will get you there...

eventually.

Pakistani Worldwide Airways

Flying you somewhere since 1956

In event of emergency

EMERGENCY EXIT

Any Indians will be ejected

Keep animals in overhead lockers

No staring at air hostesses (and the male ones)

No picking toenails. Especially your own.

No praying in aisles unless we are crash landing

No dancing at any time

The small room at the back of the plane is a toilet.

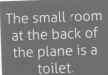

Remove shoes on slide (just like at mosque)

Emergency hijabs

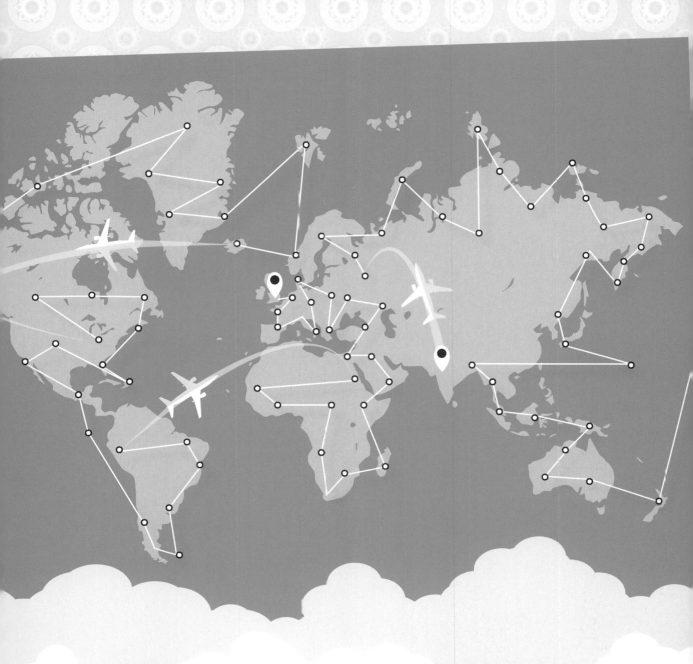

The benefit of flying with Pakistani Worldwide Airways is that even if you just buy a ticket from Karachi to London you still end up with a round the world trip. When I came, we made 78 stops and landed after 3½ months.

Upon arriving into Britain, dealing with Immigration can be the greatest challenge of them all.

They do ask a lot of questions, and you have to be very careful how to answer them. Here's what happened when I arrived into London Heathrow in 1979.

Welcome to Heathrow BAA

Me: *Asalaam Alaikum.*

Immigration Officer: Good Morning.

Me: *Asalaam Alaikum.*

IO: What is your name?

Me: No English.

IO: Where are your travelling from?

Me: No English.

IO: What are you reasons for coming to the UK?

Me: No English.

IO: Are you Pakistani?

Me: No English.

IO: You are English?

Me: No English.

IO: Do you want an interpreter?

Me: Yes.

IO: Pardon?

Me: No English.

(The immigration officer called for an interpreter. The interpreter, a Pakistani, arrived.)

IO:	Can you ask this man what his name is?
Interpreter:	OK. Hello sir. What is your name?
IO:	In Urdu!
Interpreter:	Oh, yes. [In Urdu]: Hello sir, what is your name?
Me:	[In Urdu] Mr Khan, from Gujranwala. Son of Mr Senior Khan from Gujranwala.
Interpreter:	[In Urdu] Hang on, are you from that idiot family? That boy who was born in the middle of the street?
Me:	[In Urdu] Yes.
Interpreter:	[In Urdu] Oh my god. We live in the village down the road. We are family! We have laughed about you for years, gutter boy! Will you come home and have dinner with us?
Me:	[In Urdu] Yes, if you can get me through immigration!
IO:	What's he saying? Why is here?
Interpreter:	Oh, he's seeking asylum. He's gay and is persecuted by his people. If he was to go back they would chop him up into little pieces.

(At this point I smiled and fluttered my eyelids.)

IO:	Oh well, we can't have that now can we, sweetcheeks. Come on through my gate, you naughty boy!

(The Immigration man then kissed me on the cheek and let me pass.)

Me:	Thank you. Are they always so friendly?
Interpreter:	Only to the handsome ones.

I've Arrived!

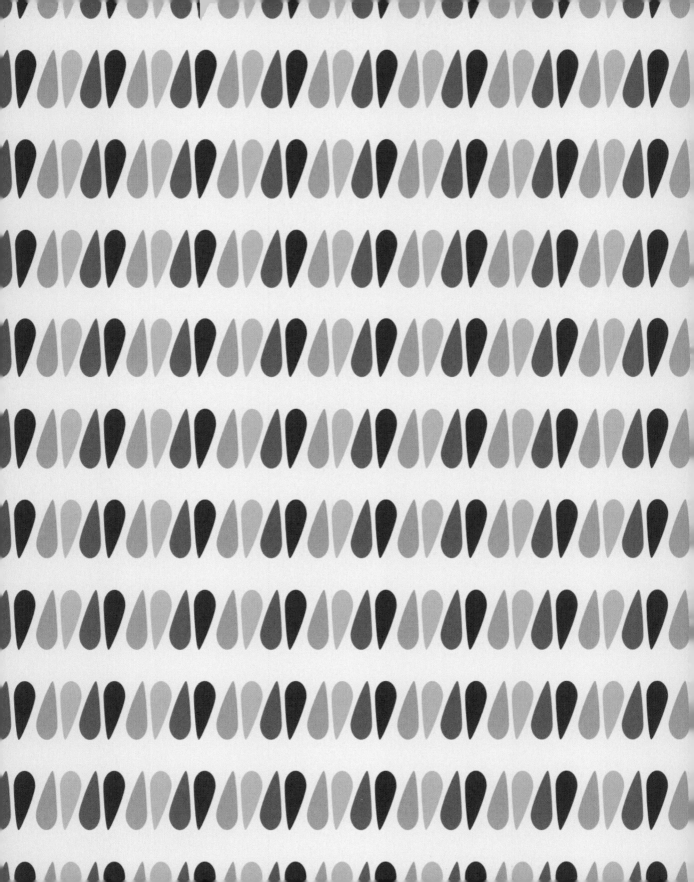

Food

Food: Improving British cuisine

There is a famous Urdu saying in Pakistan: 'If there is something out there which is good, you need to try and make it gooder'. Apple Chairman Steve Jobbys was exactly the same – he took the mobile phone and made you touch the screen with your finger – and as a Community Leader I am also going to enhance your dishes by giving them the finger.

Here are my own culinary improvements to your boring dishes.

FISH 'N' CHIPS

We all know when you order Fish and Chips at your local 'Chippie' that asking for curry sauce over your meal makes all the difference. But shock horror! It isn't proper curry. Try pouring Chicken Karahi over it instead.

BEANS ON TOAST

When times are hard every family needs to make some savings; eating beans on toast can help. In our house, we make savings on Mondays, Tuesdays, Wednesdays, Thursdays, Fridays, Saturdays and Sundays. Mrs Khan often conjures up this classic. However, to make it tastier curry would not go amiss.

FULL ENGLISH BREAKFAST

No thank you, how about a full Pakistani breakfast . . . I forget you British people won't know what this is. Basically it's the same but no silly sausages and no bloomin' bacon and a lot tastier. Now you tell me what looks better? Exactly. If you disagree, check that you are not related to Nigel Farage.

CORNFLAKES

This is traditionally eaten at breakfast time, but in the Khan household it is known as 'Khan flakes' and the dish can be eaten at anytime. You can even have this for dinner; just add hot milk over the crispy golden flakes instead.

ST CLEMENT'S PIE

At some silly fête at the community centre recently they had a stall offering many desserts and I discovered something called St Clement's Pie. This pie of yours consists of oranges and lemons and even has its own nursery rhyme telling children to chop each others heads off. What is this barbaric behaviour? So, of course, I changed it by adding Pakistani mangoes and changing the lyrics to the rhyme.

Oranges and Mangoes,
Say the bells of Fandango.
You owe me five paands
Say the bells of St Khan's
When will you pay me?
Say the bells of Rawalpindi.
When I grow rich,
Say the bells of Gilgit.
When will that be?
Say the bells of Mianwali
I do not know,
Says the great bell of Lucknow.
Here comes a candle to light you to bed.
Well don't bother, turn the Ikea lamp on instead.

This updated and improved dish with a new friendlier poem is now available in many schools in Sparkhill and is known as St Khan's Pie.

WELSH RAREBIT

You Welsh people eat anything, don't you, but unfortunately I have had to adapt your cheese toasty by taking out the rarebit. How can you eat a poor Welsh rarebit? Also I am replacing the mustard with curry.

So coming to Britain was a wonderful thing, but very quickly when I arrived I realised all was not well. Don't get me wrong. I love Britain, for many reasons (I can't think of them now) but I realised that the food is inedible for my peoples. Your dishes are simply incompatible with our way of life. Everything has got bloomin' pig in it! If you're not eating pig, you're doing something strange with it, like those people at some Oxford club.

Let me explain:

BACON BUTTY

The bacon butty is the staple diet of football fans, white van drivers, northern students and scaffolders. But not Muslims. We would be left with this:

BANGERS AND MASH

They tell me bangers and mash is one of your family favourites. Well, not in the Khan household. We end up with this. The only banger near me is next door's Vauxhall Vectra.

TOAD IN THE HOLE

Firstly, what a stupid name for food, and misleading under the Trades Description Act. Can you believe there is no bloomin' hole in this dish, you have to make it yourself... What's the bloomin' point. Oh and I am not eating a toad! I don't even know if they are halal! We Muslims can only eat the hole.

SPOTTED DICK

NO! THANK YOU! YOU PEOPLE DISGUST ME.

BUBBLE & SQUEAK

I thought this was the name of ITV's new kid's TV presenters but no, it is your leftover food from a Sunday roast, which you have made into another meal. Where is your creativity? You see in Pakistani culture, we finish our food and any excess we throw into the neighbour's garden or give to a relative we don't like. And another thing, us Pakistanis don't eat vegetables. We're not bloomin' Indian.

BLACK PUDDING

I see we are still not done with the pork. This time you want us to eat its fat and drinks its blood.

Next you will be telling me you British people have a dish called Faggot which is made from a pig's heart and belly. *This* is the black pudding I know about. Mrs Khan's bread-and-butter burnt pudding.

Food: The best food in Britain

One of the few culinary things the English got right was the invention of the Custard Cream. Or as I like to call it, the custard creamie. It really is a marvel. For me, great inventions go in this order:

1. **CUSTARD CREAMS**
2. **PENICILLIN**
3. **THE WHEEL**
4. **EVERTHING ELSE**

But there's only one way of eating a custard cream. I am going to share this with you. You can thank me later. Actually you can thank me now by buying another copy of this book. (If you are reading someone else's copy, clear off!)

Mr Khan's guide to eating a custard creamie.

(Fig.1)

(Fig.2)

(Fig.3)

(Fig.4)

STEP 1. Make a note of sell-by date in shop and purchase for bargain price on day it's out of date.

STEP 2. Make sure nobody is in the house and remove secret stash from toolbox.

STEP 3. Slowly remove one custard cream from packet. Careful not to waste any crumbs.

STEP 4. Gently tap custard cream into your hand to remove any sprinkly crumbs (Fig.1). Eat them.

STEP 5. Now this is tricky. Gently move one of the biscuit sides. So that it comes away completely without breaking (Fig.2).

STEP 6. You should now have a side of the custard cream with the beautiful cream exposed. This is the fun bit. Now lick it (Fig.3).

STEP 7. LICK IT AGAIN (Fig.3).

STEP 8. REPEAT STEP 7 (Fig.3).

STEP 9. REPEAT STEP 7 & 8 (Fig.3 & Fig.3).

STEP 10. Do not lick away all the cream. Reattach the biscuit side to the licked cream side (Fig.4) and place in biscuit tin. These can be eaten by unsuspecting mother-in-law/son-in-law.

Food: Pakistani tea

A lot of you English people like do not know how to make a simple cup of tea. You think putting a teabag in a mug, boiling a kettle, adding a splash of milk and Bob Monkhouse is your uncle. Well you are wrong. That is nas-tea. Us Pakistanis know a thing or two about tea . . . I am totally for tea. You could say I am tea-total.

At the local mosque I have created a quick instruction guide, which even a fool can follow (unless your name is Amjad) on how to make the perfect cup of tea.

HOW TO MAKE A QUICK CUP OF PAKISTANI TEA

1. Wake up at 4 a.m.
2. Brush your teeth. (You do not want any bad odour to infiltrate the tea-making process).
3. Go downstairs.
4. Open fridge door. This will also operate as a light.
5. Grab milk and smell it. If it's still liquid, go for it.
6. Get large saucepan and fill with water. Yes, a saucepan. Do as you are told.
7. Add all of milk apart from a minute drop and place back in fridge. (This saves you walking to throw an empty carton in the bin.)
8. Leave to boil gently.
9. Go back to bed.
10. Wake up and return to cooker. Water should now be a scalding 500 degrees centigrade.
11. Put ten normal-shaped tea bags into the pan (what I mean by normal is the square ones, none of the fancy hexagony pyramidy ones and ensure they are Pakistan Good Tips also known as P.G. Tips).
12. Grate some ginger and empty into pan. The root, not the minority like Dave.
13. Put 17 pieces of cloves into the pan.
14. Count 75 fennel seeds and empty into pan (any more, the tea will be spoiled and any less, the flavour of the tea will be weak).
15. Break 5 cinnamon sticks into 3 pieces each of similar length, so you have a total of 15 pieces and empty into pan.
16. Empty 5 cardamom pods into the pan. (Use green cardamom as it's the colour of the Pakistan flag so it will taste better.)
17. Treat yourself for your hard work. Eat a custard creamie.
18. Take 8 to 16 fresh mint leaves and empty into the pan. If you are allergic to mint any type of leaf will do, go into your garden and rip several leaves off a branch, wash with fairy liquid and stick in the pan. Same thing.
19. Have another custard creamie.
20. Double-check the cooker heat is now at its highest (I say this because you may be half-asleep and forget.)
21. Blow on top of the pan until you see the contents of the pan drift slightly east in the direction of Mecca. (I told you brushing your teeth is important.)
22. Put a minimum of 10 tablespoons of sugar into the pan and stir. In Pakistani culture we never ask guests how many sugars they would like and whether they have type–2 diabetes or not as it is considered rude.
23. Now simply pour into a saucer and drink. Yes, of course it's a saucer. It's so hot how do you expect to drink it? Are you bloomin' crazy? *

PUBLISHER'S NOTE:
Don't try this at home.

There you go, it's pretty simple really. This is also how the Queen drinks her tea. Why do you think she has a butler? Because she can't run downstairs at 4 a.m. at her age, can she? This is the Pakistani way of making the perfect cup of tea. There is a saying: 'Once you go Pak, you won't go back.' So why not try one today? (I'm referring to the tea.)

*To learn how to drink properly, please read the next section and while you are reading, don't forget to put the gas hob back on full heat allowing the tea to boil for longer. You don't bloomin' want cold tea now, do you?

HOW TO DRINK YOUR PERFECT SAUCER OF PAKISTANI TEA

Congratulations, you have finally made proper Pakistani tea following my quick guide, but now you need to learn how to drink the damn thing properly without burning your entire mouth.

1. Pour the tea from the pan directly into a cup.

2. Carry the tray to your preferred seating area and place on a table (Careful: the tea is hot. I get Mrs Khan to do this bit).

3. Gently pour some of the tea from the cup onto the saucer.

4. Hold the saucer with your right hand and bring it your mouth.

5. Blow onto the surface of the saucer several times, each time bringing it closer and closer to your mouth, and sip. It is Pakistani etiquette to slurp with each sip. Some people say slurping is cooling mechanism to reduce the temperature of the tea, but this is lie, as everyone knows the Pakistani tongue is non-flammable.

6. Finally, Pakistani tea is best enjoyed while watching the *Citizen Khan* DVD box set, otherwise the taste will be lacklustre. Box sets available online from Amazon at £19.99. Please don't by fake ones from Mr Lo on the high street. Buy from Mr Kadoogoo instead – he's sharing the profits with me.

CURRY CHANGED BRITAIN FOR EVER

As we know Britain was a very miserable place before curry arrived. I am not surprised. Just how much hotpot and sausages can one country eat? Here it is before curry arrived.

BRITAIN PRE-CURRY PERIOD

BRITAIN POST-CURRY PERIOD

It's clear to see the difference. The impact we have had on the streets of the UK is enormous. Look.

UK STREET BEFORE CURRY

UK STREET AFTER CURRY

In fact, in Birmingham the home of the Balti and what we call capital of curry, we have already made a few changes. The road network formerly known as Spaghetti Junction is now Curry Junction.

Curry became such a phenomenon in the UK over the years that people have really taken to it. Like this man.

MP Eric Pickles there. Even changing his surname to his favourite condiment to accompany a good curry.

But remember, not all curry is good. Some can make you feel a bit sicky. Like this one.

But all in all it's fair to say curry is now a national institution. So much so that some businesses that don't even sell curry want to be associated with it.

That is considered advertising. So, Currys head office, if you are reading this I will be coming for my payment very soon.

Food: The curry house

Many people ask me if it is true that all Pakistanis in this country have either worked as waiters or taxi drivers. That is not true and it is a complete generalisation. 99 per cent of Pakistanis might have done that, but I know of at least three Pakistanis who have worked as toilet attendants. Even me, your esteemed community leader, once worked in a Pakistani restaurant. But I wasn't a waiter! I was the Chef. And let me tell you, in my kitchen it wasn't a case of too many chefs not enough Indians! I was the boss. Then again, we could have done with a few more Indians to do the cleaning. Here's a rare photo from 1982 when I was working at a restaurant in Birmingham.

'A young Delia would often pop in to learn how to cook curry from me. Her shirt went on to inspire the colour of my Mercedes.'

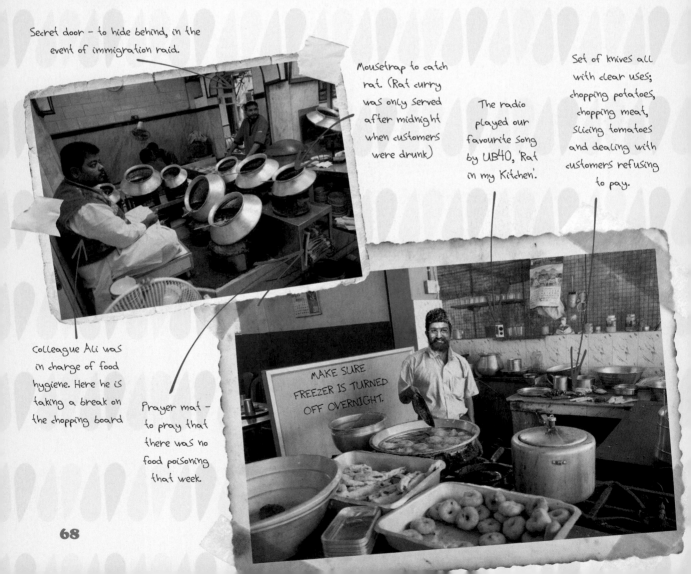

Secret door – to hide behind, in the event of immigration raid.

Mousetrap to catch rat. (Rat curry was only served after midnight when customers were drunk)

The radio played our favourite song by UB40, 'Rat in my Kitchen'.

Set of knives all with clear uses; chopping potatoes, chopping meat, slicing tomatoes and dealing with customers refusing to pay.

Colleague Ali was in charge of food hygiene. Here he is taking a break on the chopping board

Prayer mat – to pray that there was no food poisoning that week.

MAKE SURE FREEZER IS TURNED OFF OVERNIGHT.

CURRY FOR WHITE PEOPLE

An Englishman likes to eat a good curry after a good night out or after a bout of good old-fashioned hooliganism. But how does one make the perfect curry for this type of person? Well, the common feature of a curry dish is an amalgam of spices and herbs. As we have identified previously, white people are generally not fussy when it comes to eating. They will eat anything. So, don't worry too much about the detail, just give them what they think they want.

First things first, we need a setting. In this scenario we are in an authentic curry restaurant just off the Stratford Road in Sparkhill, Birmingham, which is run and owned by the short people also known as Bengali peoples. Their height restriction is useful when they need to get under the table to place tissue under the wonky leg.

Let's imagine the customer is called 'Steve' and orders a chicken curry dish. The waiter asks, 'how would you like it?' The white person, I mean Steve, says 'I want it authentic, just like you eat it my old son', and this is where we begin.

This waiter is simply not smiling enough. He won't last 5 minutes in this business.

METHOD & INGREDIENTS

Before serving Steve his food, we must ensure the following:

- Steve is seated near the window (so other Steves can see that this restaurant is not only for brown people).

- Steve has had at least eight pints of beer before his meal is served. It may be worth giving Steve the first beer on the house. You can probably charge him at the end anyway, he won't remember.

- 10g of chicken. 100g of any other meat you can get cheap.

- 1000ml of cooking oil.

- 55 tablespoons of curry power (the cheap ones off the supermarket shelf will do, try and get the one that looks most red).

- 11 500g packets of Red Colouring Powder.

- Add 500g of Natural Yoghurt (good chance to get rid of out-of-date pot).

- Add 15 tablespoons of salt. (The more salt, the more booze he will drink).

- Throw everything together in a pan and let it cook for 8–10 minutes on full heat.

- Once done and everything is red, add more red colouring: 1 more 250g packet of Red Colouring Powder should be just about enough.

- Now time for the magic ingredient which makes everything better: Coriander. Sprinkle some coriander leaves gently on top of the curry.

- Put the serving into a metal dish — white people think we have these at home. We don't.

- Now you need to find your skinniest and shortest waiter with the best grin to hand the dish to Steve.

- The tray must be lowered onto the table while the waiter is doing the customary head bobble (swivelling of head right to left) and ensuring his teeth are on full display while also maintaining eye contact with Steve to show he is confident in the service and quality of the food.

PUBLISHER'S NOTE:
Don't try this at home.

MRS KHAN'S CHICKEN CURRY

When I first married Mrs Khan, I didn't care less if she cooked or not.
I later discovered this was a mistake. What good is a man without food?
That's like a kangaroo that doesn't hop – completely useless.

The stereotype that women should be in the kitchen for eighteen hours a
day is a completely outdated concept. I say around eleven hours is enough;
I am a very modern man. When Mrs Khan told me she wanted to go out
to work, I was very supportive. I said, 'sweeting darling, work all the hours
in the world', because someone has to pay the electricity bill and more
importantly I can watch the cricket and not have to answer ridiculous
questions such as 'Who's winning?' on the first day of a test match.

When Mrs Khan announces she is going to cook her special
chicken curry, I try to book a table at Nando's. If not, I book
a doctor's appointment for the following day.

MRS KHAN'S SPECIAL CHICKEN CURRY

METHOD and INGREDIENTS

4 large onions very roughly chopped and placed into a pan with 150ml of vegetable oil then burnt to a crisp, caused by Mrs Khan being distracted as she was face-timing her sister in Bradford.

Mrs Khan then throws in the following, not necessarily in this order:

1kg of frozen chicken thigh. As Mrs Khan has been putting the washing out she forgot to properly defrost the chicken so she places under hot tap for 10 seconds.

4 or 40 garlic cloves

4 pieces or 24 pieces of ginger

10 tablespoons of garam masala. Occasionally Mrs Khan empties the entire jar because she's too busy snap-chatting a cooking tutorial. Unlike Snapchat her food self-destructs before it's been eaten.

10 tablespoons of chilli powder

10 tablespoons of turmeric

5 kg of salt. Not to be confused with white man recipe where salt is used to get someone to drink more. This is just bad cooking.

3 whole cans of chopped tomatoes. Once, Mrs Khan even cooked the lid. So a bleeding mouth is perfectly normal if you ever come around for dinner – I looked like bloomin' Jaws from James Bond.

Cook for around 5–7 hours and forget about it, literally. Silly Mrs Khan, she was distracted by doing the hoovering, dusting and shouting at her husband. So the curry is burnt.

Served with a dollop of anger and frustration and some pitta bread.
(Mrs Khan is too lazy to make chapatti. She says her hands hurt.
Asian women will know what I'm talking about.)

PUBLISHER'S
NOTE:
Don't try this
at home.

The World's Greatest Curry – My Mum's

Almost everyone says their mother's cooking is the best. Sadly my daughters have never said that. But in my case it is absolutely true. Even the little things like a glass of tap water tasted a lot better when my mummy poured it. Her famous speciality was her chicken curry.

Here is the recipe, which I have carried with me all my life. In case I end up in some American prison and I can choose my last ever meal. As a Muslim these days, you just never know.

> PUBLISHER'S NOTE:
> DO try this at home!

Method & Ingredients

- Heat up 4 tablespoons of oil in a pan, add some cumin seed, a cinnamon stick and let it swirl for a few minutes. Put some Pakistani music on.

- Add 2 onions finely sliced and allow to cook for several minutes. Have a little dance to the music.

- Add around 2 teaspoons of garlic and ginger which have been blended into a paste and cook for a few minutes. Imagine running along the beach with a Pakistani actress or Lorraine Kelly.

- Add some ground spices: 1 teaspoon of garam masala, 1 teaspoon of turmeric, 1 teaspoon of chilli powder, 1 teaspoon of coriander powder and 1 teaspoon of salt and stir for around 30 seconds. Do this with love.

- We then need to add chopped tomatoes and cook for around 8 minutes. As soon as they are a deep red paste we can then add the chicken (Please note: when buying tomatoes, do not pick the tomatoes off the first tray rack, these have been infected by wasps and dirty hands and left for white peoples, so reach for the rack underneath for fresher ones).

- Add 1kg of the finest grade-A boneless, skinless chicken breast, cut into 2-3 centimetre chunks. Coat this in the sauce and allow to cook for 10 minutes on medium heat (When you go to your local Halal butcher, say 'Assalam Alaikum' with a smile, to be served the freshest succulent pieces of chicken).

- Add 2 tablespoons of plain yoghurt (When purchasing from your local Asian store, don't be hoodwinked by any special offers i.e. 6 pots for £1. Please note that checking the date doesn't guarantee fresh yoghurt, sometimes these buggers swap the lids. So feel free to open and take a whiff).

- Add ½ litre of fresh natural spring water (tap water will do, but my mother always wanted the best for her son).

- Cook for 5 minutes and stir to mix and bring to a simmer. Turn heat to low and cook for a further 10 minutes until the sauce thickens and serve by sprinkling chopped coriander leaves on top.

- Serve with rice, naan and chapatti, a small bowl of decorative yoghurt which includes finely cut pieces of tomato and cucumber and a plate of salad with fine slices of tomato, cucumber, lettuce, red onion and olives.

Even served in metal dish for benefit of white peoples

Sport

Sport: The invention of cricket

As we know, sport is very important in this country. I really admire this, especially when you consider how bloomin' rubbish England is at it. The problem with football, golf, rugby and tennis is that it's just not cricket. Cricket is the best game in the world. Think about it: in how many games can you have bouncers, full tosses, slips, leg slips, leg glances, balls, no balls, strokes, helmets, googlies, deep fine legs, tickles, a good length, reverse swinging and even sticky wickets? I'm getting excited just thinking about it, I don't know about you!

We Pakistani Muslims love the game so much because we bloomin' invented it. Everyone knows the rules of cricket were formed by the MCC. The Muslim Cricket Club. Even today it's very much Muslim, demonstrated by its lack of women allowed into the MCC.

There is a lot of evidence to suggest Muslims invented cricket. For example:

Number of days in a test match = 5

Number of times we pray in a day = 5

Number of pillars in Islam = 5

Number of children per single bed in a Pakistani family = 5

Why do they go off for tea so late in the afternoon? Because that's how long it has taken them to make it (see previous chapter on tea-making).

Why do they have so many breaks in play? So we can all go and pray! As shown recently by Australian cricketer David Warner.

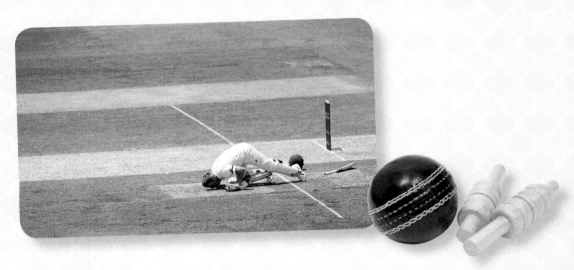

Of course one of the great early contributors to the game was a fellow Muslim:

Here he is. The Pakistani hero. Wasim Ghulam Grace.

Sport: Muslim Cricket Club

English cricket was boring when Mr Khan arrived but Pakistanis bought colour to the game.

I Know sometimes you look at me and think what would Mr Khan have been if he wasn't our brilliant Community Leader?

Well that's a difficult question to answer. I could have been a lot of things. I could have actually been a doctor. Oh yes. I was very close. When I was sixteen my father sent me to enrol at the medical school. But I was late getting there. On the way, one of the passengers on the bus I was travelling on collapsed and needed mouth-to-mouth resuscitation. All the other passengers on the bus were women so it was left to me. I got close but realised that his breath smelt worse than Mo Farah's feet after doing one of his long pointless runs! No bloomin' way I was going anywhere near that.

Anyway, I explained this to the people at the enrolment. I said 'no wonder you wear those silly masks on your face – I don't blame you!' They asked me to leave. I never heard from them again.

No wonder we got so many Indian doctors in the UK. They used to this bad breath problem, isn't it.

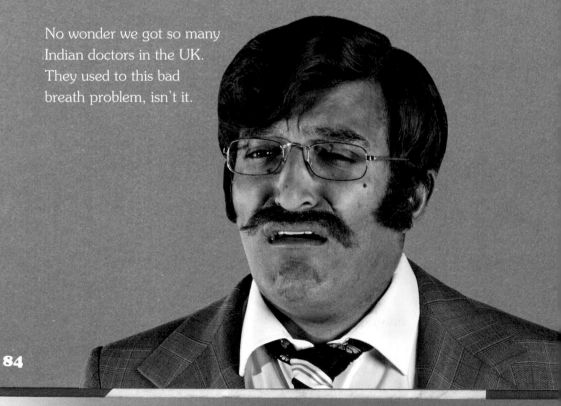

Anyway, where was I? One of the things I could have been was a cricketer. But instead I decided to pass on my expertise to my cousin, Imran Khan.

In fact I have many famous relatives. Here I am showing my nephew Amir Khan a move or two . . .

And of course I helped the career of my distant relative. Chaka Khan. Chaka Khan.

85

I was a successful cricketer in my time, though I don't like to boast. But since you ask here is one of the old scorecards when I was bowling for Gujranwala to the local team down the road.

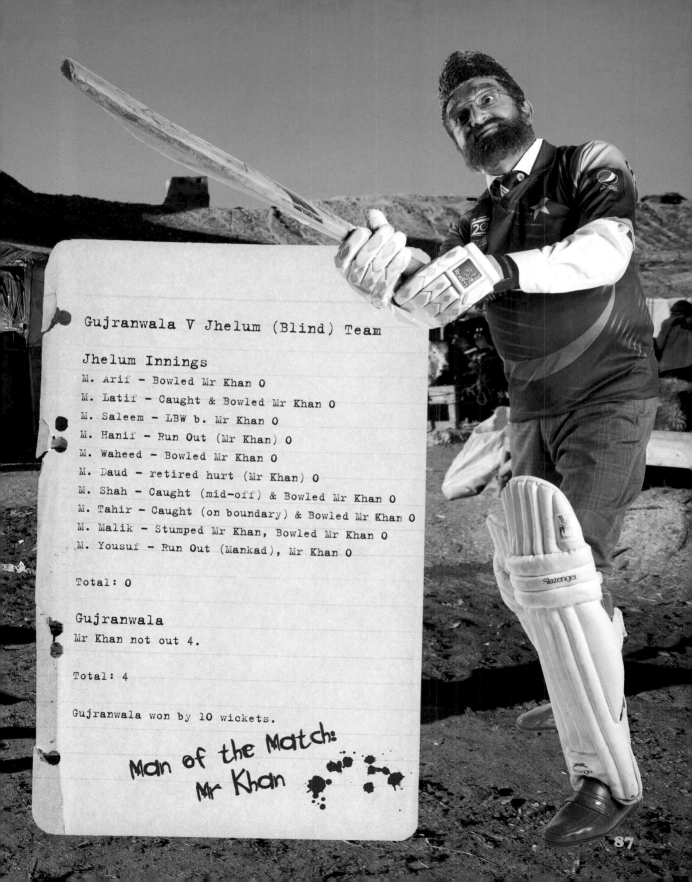

Gujranwala V Jhelum (Blind) Team

Jhelum Innings
M. Arif - Bowled Mr Khan 0
M. Latif - Caught & Bowled Mr Khan 0
M. Saleem - LBW b. Mr Khan 0
M. Hanif - Run Out (Mr Khan) 0
M. Waheed - Bowled Mr Khan 0
M. Daud - retired hurt (Mr Khan) 0
M. Shah - Caught (mid-off) & Bowled Mr Khan 0
M. Tahir - Caught (on boundary) & Bowled Mr Khan 0
M. Malik - Stumped Mr Khan, Bowled Mr Khan 0
M. Yousuf - Run Out (Mankad), Mr Khan 0

Total: 0

Gujranwala
Mr Khan not out 4.

Total: 4

Gujranwala won by 10 wickets.

Man of the Match:
Mr Khan

For many years we Pakistanis have been accused of ball tampering. But come on, honestly, what man has never tampered with his balls? It's part of life, and is nothing to be ashamed of. Quite frankly, for some guys it's the only way of getting any action on the pitch. Many of us work on each other's balls together. It's something that we should be proud of.

Tampering with the ball in cricket is known to help with the movement and swing of it. Here are some ball tampering methods to look out for:

Rubbing plenty of Vaseline on your balls can especially help swingers.

Some people like to use bottle tops. If they are having a drink and the top accidentally damages the ball then it's hardly their fault, is it?

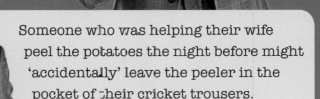

Someone who was helping their wife peel the potatoes the night before might 'accidentally' leave the peeler in the pocket of their cricket trousers.

Someone who was helping their wife with the dishes the night before might 'accidentally' leave the scourer in the pocket of their cricket trousers.

Someone who was helping their wife plastering the kitchen walls the night before might 'accidentally' leave the sander in the pocket of their cricket trousers.

PAKISTANI RULES OF CRICKET

Over the years cricket has changed very much.
For example these days we have Twenty20 cricket. Designed to bring plenty of joy and plenty of money to those that are part of it! We have seen the same thing happen in Pakistani cricket. Let me give you example:

In Pakistani cricket

- You hit ball to boundary you get 4 runs
- You hit ball to boundary without bouncing you get 6 runs
- You bowl a no ball you get £20,000 and a Rolex watch

In English cricket the biggest prize that you can win is the Ashes. I know it's difficult to see but that brown dot is the trophy the British and Australians are desperate to win. Which would you prefer?
I rest my case your honour!

Anyway, you may find that some cricketers attempt a bit of sledging – basically this means putting the batsman off. This is not acceptable. Here are some examples of when that might have happened in Pakistani cricket but with quite simple explanations.

It's not my fault my phone rang. I was waiting for a call from Kwik Fit to say my MOT had been done.

It's very normal for Pakistanis to have two jobs. As we can see here I was practicing for my orchestra rehearsals that evening. Fair enough.

Of course it's very important that we are allowed to pray when we need to. If this particular time was when the game was getting away from us then that is merely a coincidence.

Spot the Difference

Moeen Ali

W G Grace

(This is a trick – there aren't any!)

Many people say to me 'why do you support Pakistan and not England?' Well, I just say, 'I am practicing for the day when I will support England.' As in, the future England team will all be Pakistani. In fact the future England XI could look like this:

1. Ali Stewart

2. Mark Halal Butcher

3. Kevin Pakistanison

4. Allan Lamb Seekh Kebab

5. Mike Beardley

6. Geoff Mullah

7. Ian Halal Beefy Botham

8. Chris Read Your Prayers

9. Robin Jack Pakistaniman

10. Ghulam Dilley

11. Devon Malikom

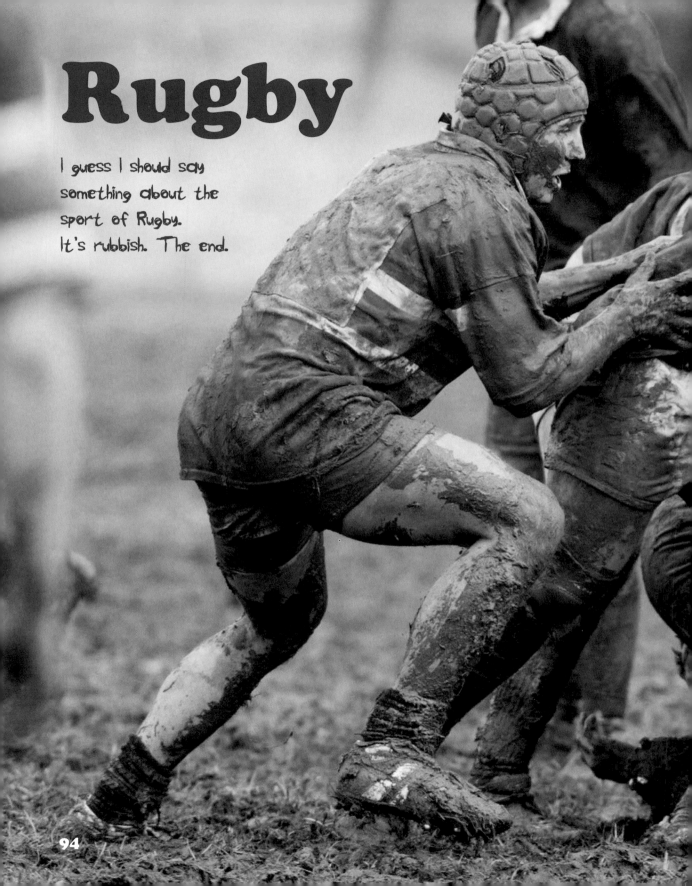

Rugby

I guess I should say something about the sport of Rugby. It's rubbish. The end.

94

Sometimes in sport when a team does very badly it's time for a complete overhaul — some clever restructuring needs to take place at the club. For example in my home city of Birmingham, Aston Villa found themselves relegated to the Championship from the Premier League. As community leader I popped in to see them and offered up my plan:

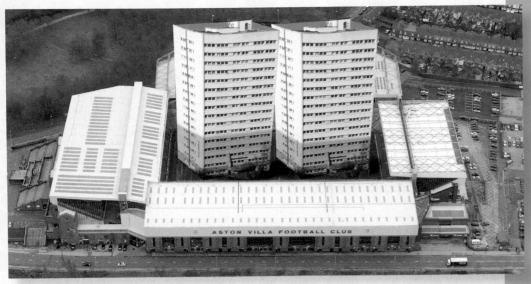

This will greatly solve the housing problem in the area.

Also if we look at the national team of England, they are a bit rubbish too, aren't they? They couldn't even beat Iceland in the Euros! Iceland! A team from a frozen food shop! Unbelievable. Now had it been Lidl I would have understood as they're bloomin' Germans!

So it's time to put the England team and fans out of their misery and find another use for Wembley Stadium.

This would be ideal. It is already perfectly located in Wembley, where there are lots of Asians. To be honest a football stadium is a lot like a mosque. Once a week a congregation of mostly men head there to bow down and worship their God, and occasionally they might end up in a fight or two!

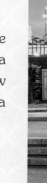

Family

Raising a family in Britain is a very good thing to do. The main reason being is that you can get income support and child benefits. At least £57 a week – imagine how many custard creamies that is. I will tell you: it's 4,543 custard creams. Oh Twaddi!

But of course it's not right to rely on child benefits to get by. At some point you need to think of work too. So do make sure your kids get a job as soon as humanly possible. It's never too young to start.

What a brilliant way of cutting the grass and at the same time teaching your baby to walk. All while you can sit back and watch the cricket.

Honestly, if Maggie Philbins was still doing *Tomorrow's World* I would be a shoo-in.

But really, families are important. Especially sons. Daughters are OK too. Once they understand the rules of cricket. It's important that you have lots of fun and happiness with your family.

Family is very important.

Here is a traditional family. Mum, Dad and two kids. Mum doing the cooking, Dad back from work and the children playing that well-known game – what can we steal from Daddy's briefcase.

Many people say that this traditional family doesn't exist anymore. They say families are different nowadays. You have step-families, single parent families and mixed-race families. Well, I say the traditional family does still exist.
Take a look overleaf.

Look at us, a very British family. You have Mum, Dad and two kids. Here you can see Alia, face-timing the Imam, and of course other daughter. Other daughter has changed a lot over the years. In fact today you could say she's a completely different person. In this photo is also son-in-law Amjad. I didn't want to scare the kids reading this book so we put a bag on his head. I think that headdress with just a little space for the eyes could catch on amongst the community – what do you think?

By the way do you like the furnishings? Yes? Thought so. Looks modern doesn't it. We could be on one of those modern property shows. You could call it *Lookasian, Lookasian, Lookasian*!

We are very similar to the traditional family in many ways. Here's the traditional family's car, and next to it, mine.

We both got nice yellow car, see! Incidentally, that's how we park in Sparkhill. What's the problem? That woman has got four wheels on that thing, she should be on the road. What next? Smart cars can go on pavement? If you have a Nissan Micra feel free to drive straight into Debenhams? No!

Please note, that is advertising for Debenhams. I will be popping into the Birmingham Bull Ring store for my 24-piece dinner set very soon.

So we all agree it's Pakistani families like mine that are maintaining this Great British tradition of family. What do you mean, no? Even the Office of National Statistics agree with me. According to their own research it is clear that we Pakistanis love families.

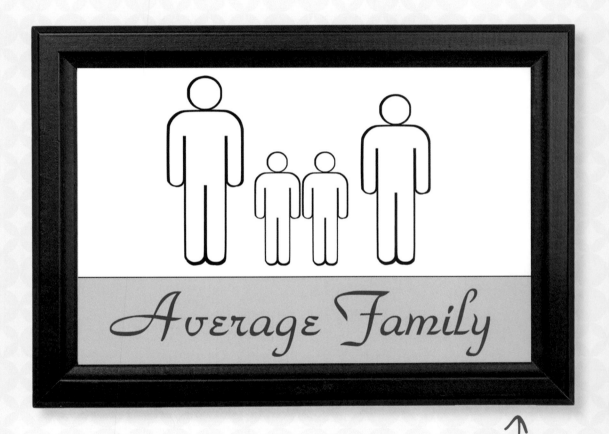

Average Family

There you are. Mum. Dad. Two kids.

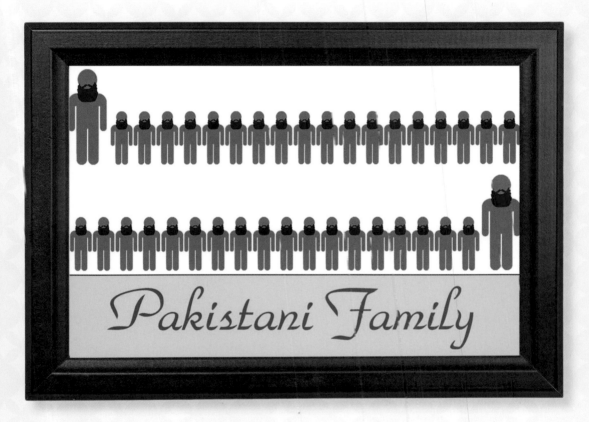

Pakistani Family

This is a family many will recognise. Even the mum at the end has a beard. In fact I know them very well. Let me introduce them. From left to right. It's Mr Ali, then we have Ali, Ali, Ali, Ali, Ali, Ali, Ali, Ali, Ali, Ali, Ali, Ali, Ali, Ali, Ali, Ali, hang on what's he called again? Oh god, what's he called? Erm, erm..? Anyway, you get the picture. But what's the name of the one on the end stood next to Mum? Ali? Of course not! That's Fatima, the daughter!

Yes, we Pakistanis are known for having large families, having arranged marriages and living all under one roof. But don't just look at us. We have learned from the best. Look. The Queen is very much like a Pakistani woman. Here she is, wearing a hijab. She very rarely leaves the house, always has a man drive her around, and like many Pakistanis she pays very little tax!

Now that's what I call a Royal Tandoori!

Family: Raising children

One of the biggest concerns when having a family is how to raise your children. It's very important that you bring them up well and teach them about all the best ways to be. Here are my top ten rules:

How to bring up the perfect daughter

1. Always carry ten pounds in your pocket. You never know when your daughter will need money for some school books. Alia always seems to ask for them very late at night. Did you know WHSmith have a 24-hour store? Me neither.

2. Be aware that it is very common for males to call the house phone very late at night to talk to your daughter. Alia tells me it's the teachers from school checking on her homework.

3. If your daughter comes in very tired at 2 or 3 in the morning, stumbling around, it's because she has been at the 24-hour library.

4. It's a good idea to send your children to Islamic Summer Camp. Next year Alia's going to one in Ibiza! She says it's just full of libraries and cafes. Very good.

5. Don't be alarmed if your daughter is on her phone all the time. She is probably just using the Call To Prayer app.

6. Be wary that your children might be prone to sleepwalking. I went downstairs for a cheeky custard creamie and bumped into Alia in her coat and heels heading out the front door. It turns out she was sleepwalking. I have seen her do this six times in the past three months, bizarrely always on Saturday nights.

7. If your daughter goes upstairs to pray, don't be surprised if she is back downstairs in less than 60 seconds. Alia is so good at it she can pray very quickly. I call her Alia Usain Bolt Khan.

8. Be warned, if you ask your daughter to recite some prayers to you she might say she is shy. Since she started learning Arabic sixteen years ago not once have I heard her recite any prayers. She says she doesn't like to show off. She is so humble.

9. You might be disturbed that your daughter is wearing very tight clothing. Don't make the mistake I made and bring it up. She asked for £100 to buy new clothes as she said these were old, hence a bit tight. I have never mentioned it again. Tight is right!

10. Do not compare your children and show preferential treatment. It's not other daughter's fault she is not as brilliant as good daughter.

Family: Days out

As a family it is important that you have days out together. So sometimes we all go into the garden.

It suits me fine, and for the mother-in-law it's even better as you are never too far from the toilet. But sometimes the family complain. They say they want to go further afield. I agree and take them to Mrs Haroon's garden two doors down. Coincidentally the grass hasn't been cut for years so it actually looks like a field.

But the family want to see new things and meet other people that are going on holiday. So I have come up with the best solution.

Here I am at Newport Pagnall service station. The perfect holiday location: there's plenty of parking, lots of food options (although it's a bit expensive so you're better off taking your own) and just like my family wanted – lots of other people who are going on holiday to meet and talk to. Many of them are off to towns in Wales and other smelly places. This way you can have a holiday without having to actually go to Wales! Bloomin' brilliant!

Family: Days out

Another top tip for having a day out with the family is taking a trip to B&Q. Honestly it's right up there with Center Parcs and all that stuff. Think about it, they got it all. Garden furniture to sit on, baths and toilets, beds and barbecues! It's like a posh Butlins. Another top tip is to tell them you are buying a bathroom and they will give you a free cup of tea or coffee. Year before last we spent the entire Bank Holiday Weekend there.

Car Showroom day out!

OK. I think some of you more fussy people need more sophisticated suggestions. That's fine, I can do sophisticated. I'm very sophisticated. I once ate five Ferrero Rocher all in one go! For you poshy types from places like Solihull etc. how about a day trip to a car showroom? That's right, take your family with you and pretend you're buying a new car.

You get to sit inside, recline the seats, put the cricket commentary on and they bring you not just tea but a hot bloomin' chocolate! We do this a lot as a family.

Jaguar even let you take the car for a test drive: I drove it to Bradford to see some relatives. The salesman got on really well with my cousin Rafiq.

I have never been to Italy. But the Ferrari show room in Sutton Coldfield was fantastic. I even ordered a pizza from Domino's for the authentic touch.

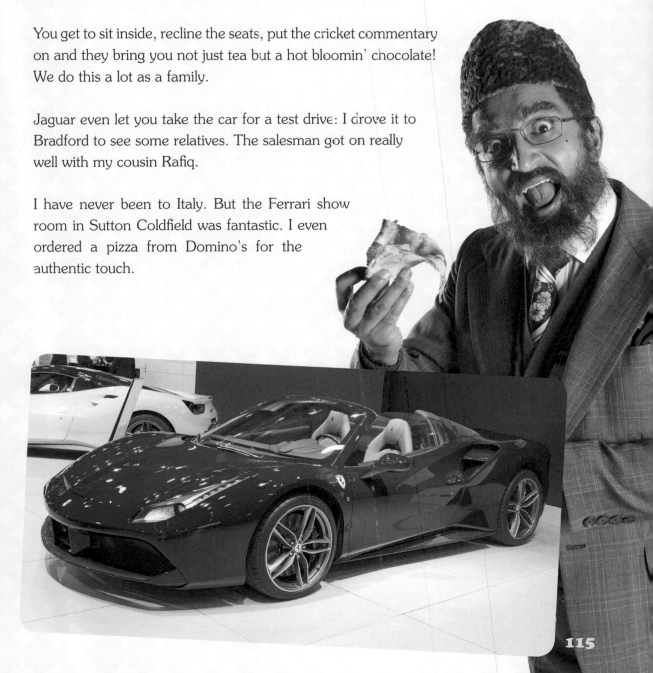

As the head of the family there is a lot that is asked of you. Like when you are asked to move your feet as the wife does the hoovering, not to put the empty milk carton back in the fridge and not to leave your toenail clippings on the kitchen sink. Honestly, all these rules! I left Pakistan because of dictatorship! But the worst thing is when you are asked to attend a family gathering. I hate them, mainly because I end up paying for them. So here are my top ten excuses for getting out of them!

Mr Khan's Top 10 excuses to AVOID family gatherings

1. My cousin in Luton is dying. I have to go and see him. He still owes me £7.50 I lent him for a train ticket to Lords in 1988.

2. My cousin in Peterborough is having marital problems. His wife says he never spends enough time at home. I am taking him to the test match to get his mind off things.

3. My cousin in Peterborough is having marital problems. Her husband never spends enough time at home I am taking her to the test match to get her mind off things. (Being Pakistani you can use cousins as an excuse a lot. You have around three thousand of them, so it's entirely plausible).

4. My cousin from Pakistan is arriving and I need to collect him from the airport.

5. My cousin who arrived from Pakistan forgot his bag at the airport so I have to go back again.

6. My cousin from Pakistan says he wants to come and stay here or I take him to London for the weekend. My cousin is called Smelly feet Faroze.

7. My cousin from Pakistan is going back to Pakistan so I need to take him to the airport.

8. My cousin forgot his bag in the UK so I have to go and drop it off to him in Pakistan.

9. My other cousin from Pakistan is arriving and I need to collect him from the airport.

   (REPEAT EXCUSES, 5,6,7,8)

10. 'No English'

Family: Communication

In any family, communication is key. This is where most families break apart, by not finding quality time to communicate. So we leave each other post-it notes on the fridge. This makes things so much easier.

Here's our latest conversation:

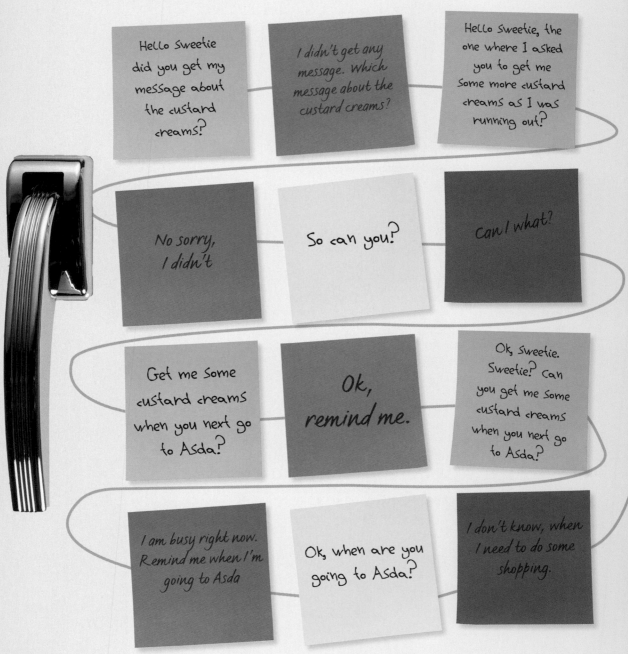

Hello sweetie did you get my message about the custard creams?

I didn't get any message. Which message about the custard creams?

Hello sweetie, the one where I asked you to get me some more custard creams as I was running out?

No sorry, I didn't

So can you?

Can I what?

Get me some custard creams when you next go to Asda?

Ok, remind me.

Ok, sweetie. Sweetie? can you get me some custard creams when you next go to Asda?

I am busy right now. Remind me when I'm going to Asda

Ok, when are you going to Asda?

I don't know, when I need to do some shopping.

When will that be?

At the weekend

Ok. I'll leave you a note to remind you.

Good idea.

Great. Actually. Do you still have the post it note?

Which one?

The one about the custard creams?

Which one about the custard creams?

The one where I asked if you could get me some more?

I thought I told you I didn't get it?

Yes I know.

So why are you asking me then?

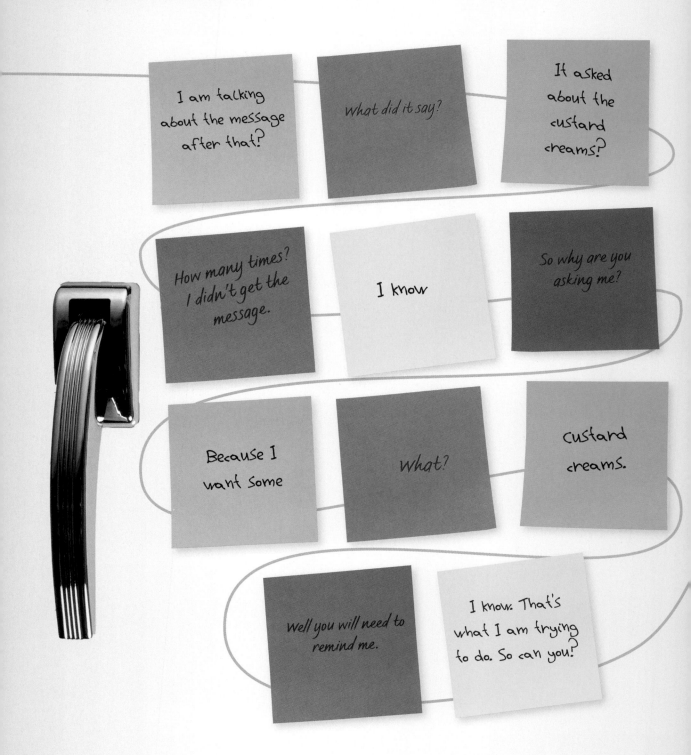

I am talking about the message after that?

What did it say?

It asked about the custard creams?

How many times? I didn't get the message.

I know

So why are you asking me?

Because I want some

What?

Custard creams.

Well you will need to remind me.

I know. That's what I am trying to do. So can you?

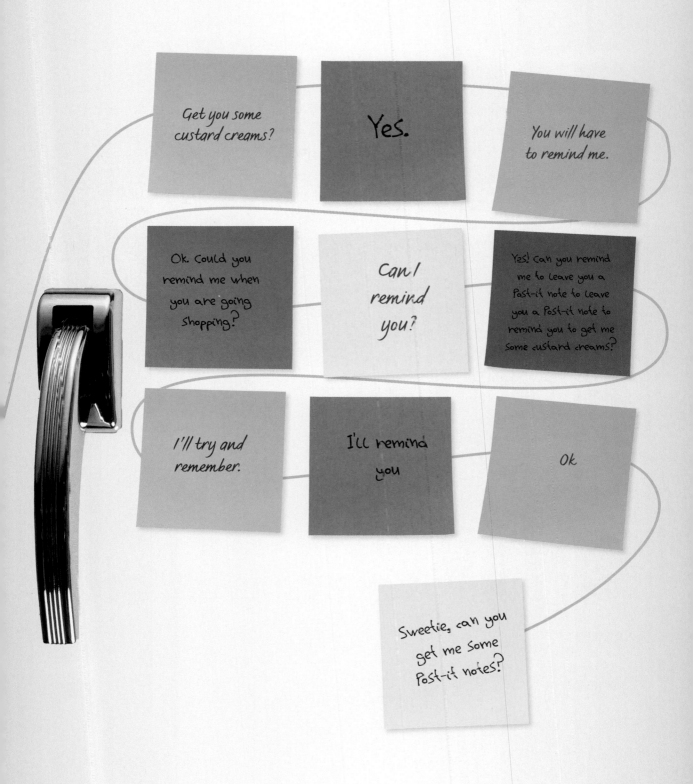

One of the most important days in a family's household is when it is someone's birthday. Just what present do you buy? Sometimes it can be so hard. But do not worry, Mr Khan is here to help. Here's what I bought for Mrs Khan's birthday for the past twenty-five years.

1992 *

1993

1994

1995

1996 *

1997

1998

1999

2000

2001 *

2002

2003

2004

2005

2006 *

2007

2008

2009

2010 *

2011

2012

2013

2014

2015

2016 *

* This birthday Mrs Khan got a smaller handbag as I needed money to buy tickets for the Pakistan cricket tour.

Marriage

In this country I have realised that many peoples have dated and had partners before they get married. People often think that we Pakistani men come from very traditional societies where we didn't even date women before marriage. Well, let me tell those people – you're absolutely right! How did you know? Yes, it was very tricky. But some of us found a way. Quite often our relationships would basically consist of staring at each other on the bus. I had one such relationship with a young girl from the next village. We dated/stared for nearly eighteen months. Be sure not to miss your stop, though. Once I stared at her so much I almost ended up in Chittagong. The trick of a good stare is not to smile. That would be creepy.

These are quite good relationships really. You just stare, don't have to talk to each other, and don't have to pay for her food and shoes, etc.

My cousin Ali in his first relationship. His stare lasted 7 years.

What a stare!
Enough to get
any lady excited!

Never let it be said that Mr Khan isn't a romantic. From the very beginning of our relationship I would exchange love letters with Mrs Khan. When I say letters, I would pass little notes to her when I used to see her on the bus. This used to be our version of WhatsApp.

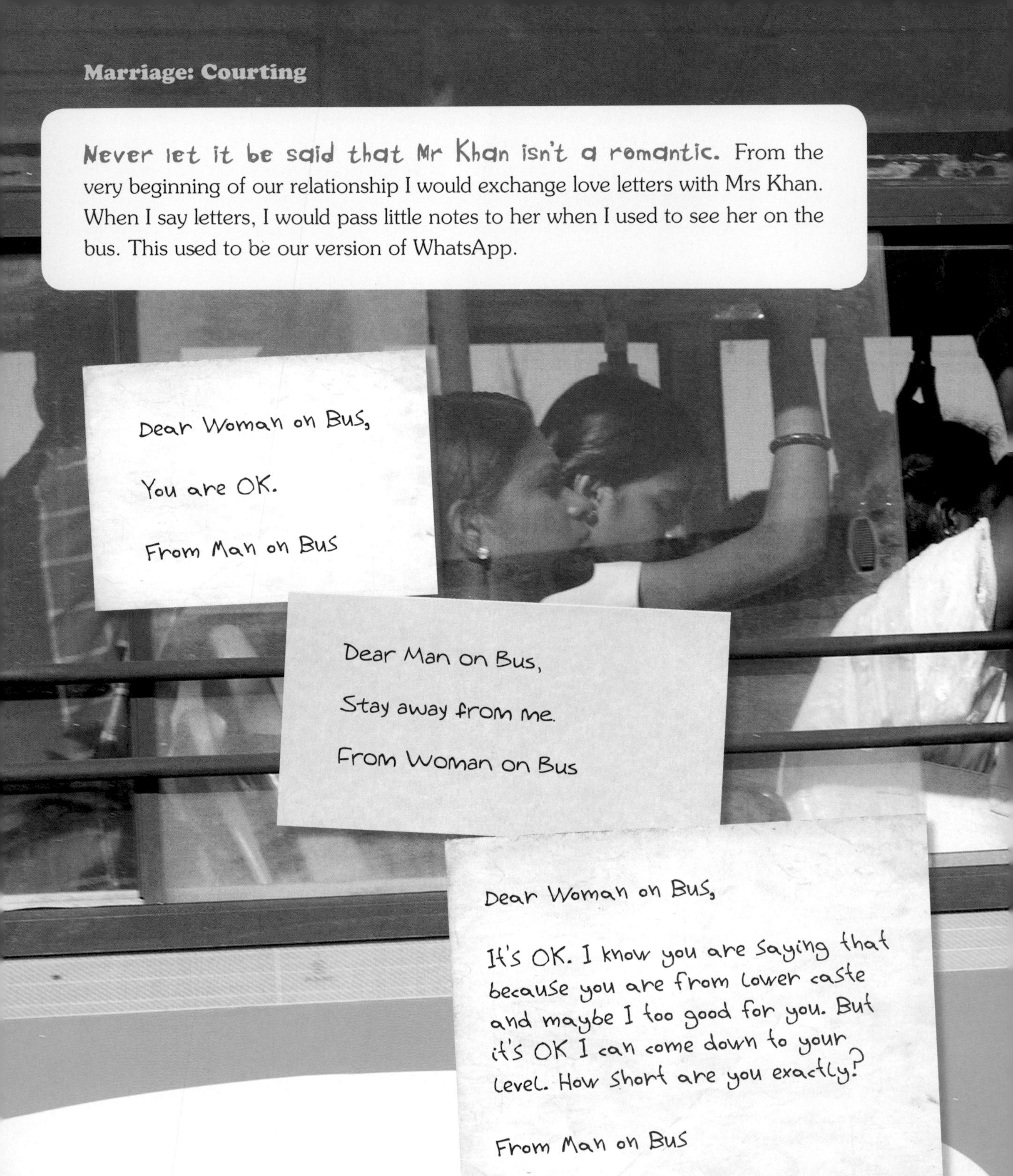

Dear Woman on Bus,

You are OK.

From Man on Bus

Dear Man on Bus,

Stay away from me.

From Woman on Bus

Dear Woman on Bus,

It's OK. I know you are saying that because you are from lower caste and maybe I too good for you. But it's OK I can come down to your level. How short are you exactly?

From Man on Bus

Dear Man on Bus,

If you come anywhere near me I might do something I might regret.

From Woman on Bus

Dear Woman on Bus,

I understand. But there is nothing to be ashamed of. My aunty says that all the time to my uncle. They have ended up having eleven children. Enough for a whole cricket team.

From Man on Bus

Dear Man on Bus,

Listen. I don't play games.

From frustrated Woman on Bus

Dear Woman on Bus,

Well maybe you should play games. You can begin by coming to watch me at the weekend if you like? I am very good with my balls and many people have commented on my in-swinger. Then later you can see me get my bat out and stroke it through the covers? What do you say?

From Man on Bus

I was banned by the conductor from ever catching that bus again.

This is the carriage I used to take Mrs Khan home on our wedding night.

When we Pakistani people get married, a question is always asked. Was it a love marriage or an arranged marriage? Quite frankly, it's none of your bloomin' business, but in the case of this book I will tell you they are both the same. A death sentence.

However, there are a lot of benefits in having an arranged marriage. The main one is that to arrange this type of marriage you don't have to do anything apart from going to a few houses for free cups of tea and cake. Basically, you just turn up on the day of the wedding and Bob's your bride (and he may also be your uncle, if you're Pakistani).

Let me explain the process. The groom-to-be visits a girl's house with his parents. The families talk about all types of thing e.g. 'What car does the boy drive?' 'How big is the boy's car?' 'How big are the boy's earnings?' 'How big are his feet?' And so on. After an awkward silence, the boy and girl are allowed to go into another room (not the bedroom) to talk privately for a few minutes. This conversation is usually silent, and just as the boy is about to talk, the girl's family come in to the room to check 'everything is OK' – and the meeting is over. The next time you meet will be in the banqueting suite when you are getting married.

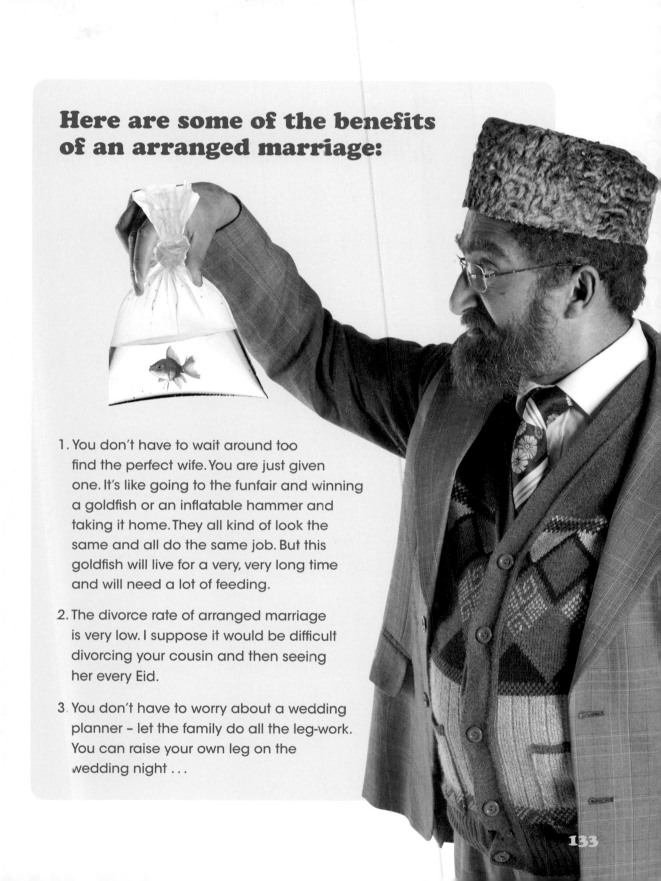

Here are some of the benefits of an arranged marriage:

1. You don't have to wait around too find the perfect wife. You are just given one. It's like going to the funfair and winning a goldfish or an inflatable hammer and taking it home. They all kind of look the same and all do the same job. But this goldfish will live for a very, very long time and will need a lot of feeding.

2. The divorce rate of arranged marriage is very low. I suppose it would be difficult divorcing your cousin and then seeing her every Eid.

3. You don't have to worry about a wedding planner – let the family do all the leg-work. You can raise your own leg on the wedding night . . .

Admittedly, there comes a time in any marriage that you might find the need to spend some of your hard-earned money on romantic breaks. Romantic break-the-bank more like! Someone said to me the other day 'oh, me and my wife went to Paris last week, it was very romantic'. Very romantic? Sounds 'very expensive' to me.

Well, I have come up with some alternative suggestions.

If you do like I do, you can experience Paris without even going outside the UK. It means you don't have to have their smelly food, and anyway, we aren't part of the EU any more, so stay clear, I say. If you take the Blackwall tunnel in London, find a big electric pylon like I did and tell the wife it's the Eiffel Tower, she'll be none the wiser.

You know Kate and Willy? They went to India recently. The must have got lost on their way to a much better place – Pakistan. Well, they had a photo taken outside the Taj Mahal. So bloomin' what? So did Mrs Khan and I, in Birmingham.

Similarly, many people go to Venice to get all romantic on the canals. Well, we have more canals than Venice in Birmingham, so I took Mrs Khan there instead.

By the way, I get fed up of that 'more canals than Venice' line about Birmingham. We really need something else. So I have suggested to the tourism department that we use this instead.

(Note: Since the city is soon to become majority Muslim we are getting rid of the 'ham'.)

More mosques than Karachi!

137

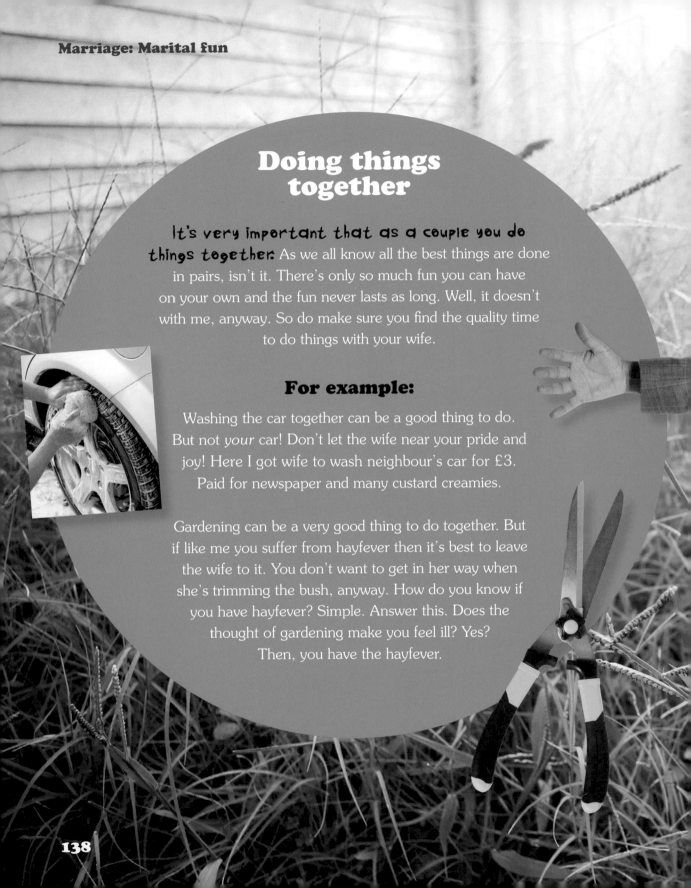

Doing things together

It's very important that as a couple you do things together. As we all know all the best things are done in pairs, isn't it. There's only so much fun you can have on your own and the fun never lasts as long. Well, it doesn't with me, anyway. So do make sure you find the quality time to do things with your wife.

For example:

Washing the car together can be a good thing to do. But not *your* car! Don't let the wife near your pride and joy! Here I got wife to wash neighbour's car for £3. Paid for newspaper and many custard creamies.

Gardening can be a very good thing to do together. But if like me you suffer from hayfever then it's best to leave the wife to it. You don't want to get in her way when she's trimming the bush, anyway. How do you know if you have hayfever? Simple. Answer this. Does the thought of gardening make you feel ill? Yes? Then, you have the hayfever.

Yes, yes, I know what you are thinking. You should do something more physical together. OK. How about this:

This day was so much fun. I was ecstatic. The cricket commentary was on the radio. Pakistan beat England by seven wickets!

Marriage: Tang tang

All right, all right, keep your knickers on. You want me to talk about the 'you know what'. What I like to call tang tang. Yes of course we all have to do this from time to time, in order to have the children or in some instances to have the food on the table.

If the brothers from the Mosque are reading this, please turn the page now. Actually, turn to next chapter. Thank you.

So here goes. Once you are in bedroom, here is my three-step plan:

STEP ONE

STEP

LIGHTS OFF

TANG

TWO

STEP THREE

TANG

LIGHTS ON,
CUPPA TEA

Marriage

DATE OF MARRIAGE	1 April 1988
NAMES:	Mr Khan
ADDRESS:	In Cousin's Spare Bed
AGE:	~~█~~
CONDITION:	Disturbed
OCCUPATION:	Any day now
FATHER'S NAME AND SURNAME:	Mr Khan
FATHER'S PROFESSION:	Community Leader

WITNESSES:

Man Having Cigarette Outside

Woman Who Was With Man Having Cigarette Outside

Certificate

Mrs Razia Noor

On Cousin's Sofa

Over 16

Distraught

Housewife

Disowned Daughter

Recently A Hit Man

Education

One of the biggest problems we face in this country is the standard of education. It really is a problem. Too many children want to grow up to be famous peoples. This sounds so irresponsible to me, they should think of being something more important, like a Community Leader. Except not in Sparkhill, you can clear off. Being a Community Leader is very

	7 am	8 am	9 am	10 am	11 am	12.00 - 12.05pm
MONDAY	Islamic Studies	Islamic Studies	Cricket	Islamic Studies	Islamic Studies	Lunch
TUESDAY	Geography	Islamic Studies	Art	Islamic Studies	Islamic Studies	Lunch
WEDNESDAY	Islamic Studies	History	Maths	Islamic Studies	IT	Lunch
THURSDAY	Islamic Studies	Islamic Studies	History	Islamic Studies	Islamic Studies	Lunch
FRIDAY	Home Economics	Islamic Studies	Islamic Studies	Art	Geography	Lunch

important. Above all else, you get to call yourself a Community Leader. There's possibly only one thing better than a Community Leader and that's a Pakistani Muslim Community Leader. So in our education system we need to make sure young children grow up be more like me. Yes, that's right. Mr Khan is putting the Asian back into Educasian! Here is a typical day in Mr Khan's Academy:

12.05 pm	2 pm	3 pm	4 pm	5 pm	6 pm	7 pm
Islamic Studies	Home Economics	Islamic Studies	History	Islamic Studies	Science	Islamic Studies
Islamic Studies	History	Maths	Maths	Islamic Studies	Cricket	Cricket
Islamic Studies	IT	Islamic Studies	Islamic Studies	Home Economics	Islamic Studies	Islamic Studies
Islamic Studies	Science	Islamic Studies	History	Islamic Studies	Cricket	Islamic Studies
Islamic Studies	Islamic Studies	Maths	Islamic Studies	Islamic Studies	Maths	Maths

HISTORY

History is an important aspect of understanding the human race and its evolution. From the greatest achievement ever which was Pakistan becoming world cricket champions in 1992 – to the invention of the filet-o-fish meal made exclusively for Muslims.

However, since arriving in England and studying all your history books, I realised a few important things were distorted or missing. So here are the top five educational things you should know.

Henry the Eighth (VIII)

The King of England was the first Muslim to rule this great country in the sixteenth century, and certainly not the last. You have another Muslim ruling London at the moment, a Mayor or something. Henry had clear Pakistani traits: he struggled a few times to have a son (a bit like me); he had a strong beard (a bit like me); wore the customary religious hat (a bit like me), and he had six wives (Are you stupid? Mrs Khan would kill me!). Also he was overweight and didn't exercise, like your typical Pakistani newsagent proprietor.

Henry the Eighth is a true Pakistani.

The first mosque in Britain

The Shah Jahan Mosque in Woking was the first mosque, built in 1889. It is situated on Oriental Road, which sounds very Chinese, and guess which country is next to China? Pakistan of course.

The Pakistan Cricket tour

The Pakistani cricket team first toured England in 1954. This is a key moment in British history as Pakistan was the first side to win a test on its inaugural visit. This was a genuine victory, as match-fixing wasn't invented then.

Transportation

England is renowned for its colonial adventurers – welcomed by the indigenous population wherever they went – especially the Pakistanis. Thanks to the British, we no longer have to live with the Indians. The British provided great infrastructure, long winding roads, bridges which stretched for miles, and of course their Victorian architecture is

to be marvelled at. But there was one more thing the British gave the world which they could only do with the help of the Pakistanis. And that is the best transport system in the world, connecting cities, towns and countries together. Of course I am talking about the taxi. Without us Pakistanis, how would you get home from clubbing? Whose car seat would you cover in sick after a few too many alcopoppys? How would you get to job centre? How would you take your shopping home from Asda? How could you ever do anything in life? God bless the Pakistani taxi-driver and their fluctuating rates.

Spaghetti Junction

Or, as we call it now, Curry Junction (see Food chapter).
One of the best motorway junctions in the United Kingdom was officially opened in 1972, connecting the city of Birmingham for the growing Pakistani population so they could visit other Pakistanis in Bradford, Manchester and Luton. It is very Islamic. This is evident because there are five different levels to the interchange. And how many times a day do Muslims pray? Five times. You see, this number five is all symbolic. Other examples include the Jazz classic by Dave Brubeck 'Take Five'– or that other famous song, 'I got five on it'. Even when peoples high-five this is about praying to the almighty high in the sky. This is all about praying. Spaghetti is probably Pakistani too, same number of letters.

GEOGRAPHY

Britain is a charming place with many beauty spots, from Birmingham Central Mosque and Drayton Manor theme park to the brown cliffs of Dover (it's on the opposite side) – you would know that if you paid attention and didn't bugger off to Tenerife every bloomin' month. Now that Britain has decided to leave the European Union (which means no more random German names on our roundabouts), it is the perfect opportunity to develop our major landmarks, which quite frankly are becoming a bit dull.

Green Belt

The main principal of a Green Belt is to keep areas permanently open and prevent development. This is a contradiction, as a Mosque is permanently open but is in constant need of development. So we need to have a rethink on the development restriction. I'm sure Shaun the Sheep and his buddies won't mind if there was a place of worship or two, or three or four. OK, seven. And that's it!

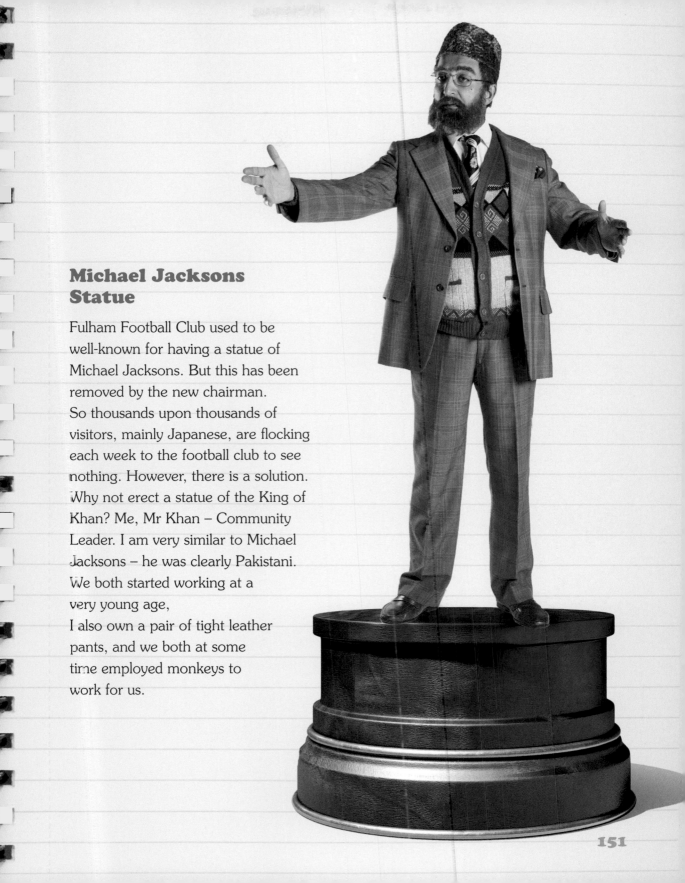

Michael Jacksons Statue

Fulham Football Club used to be well-known for having a statue of Michael Jacksons. But this has been removed by the new chairman. So thousands upon thousands of visitors, mainly Japanese, are flocking each week to the football club to see nothing. However, there is a solution. Why not erect a statue of the King of Khan? Me, Mr Khan – Community Leader. I am very similar to Michael Jacksons – he was clearly Pakistani. We both started working at a very young age, I also own a pair of tight leather pants, and we both at some time employed monkeys to work for us.

Stonehenge

Anyone with a half a brain knows that this is an uncompleted building project. There was probably some kind of recession 5,000 years ago, so construction came to a halt. The foundation has already been set – all we need to do is get some plasterboard, install a few windows, a roof and of course a minaret – and Bob's your Builder. This will make the area a more attractive place for everyone to visit, not just for rich white people that make their own jams.

Loch Ness

There is no bloomin' monster, just lots of people taking pictures of water. Now, I know what you are thinking? Mr Khan wants to build a mosque in the water! Well not quite. How about a Mosque Boat instead? This will enable the visitors to pray to God when they see the Loch Ness Monster. And if they see it, they can also pray to God – that it goes away. Just remember to dress appropriately when visiting the Loch Ness Mosque. A Burkhini will be fine.

Home Economics

HOW TO COOK THE PERFECT CHAPATTI

One of the key things we should learn in cookery class is how to cook the perfect chapatti.
The Chapatti, also known as 'Roti', is a type of flatbread. It is the perfect accompaniment to any food. In my culture, a woman is judged on the roundness of her chapattis. Most men like them big, round, and soft. I am very much in the category of most men, but don't get me wrong, I understand the pressures of the modern women. With their busy hectic lifestyles, buying shoes and gossiping, they have become out of shape. If they follow my guide, we can all enjoy round chapattis once more.

Instructions

1. Use good quality wheat flour. Available from my cousin's shop in Sparkhill, 2 for the price of 3 offer on now.

2. You need to have the right mix of water in ratio to the flour, i.e. 2 cups of flour = 1 cup of water. Also have nice mix of Pakistani songs on the radio.

3. Wet the flour and keep kneading until soft – press down hard with your fists. You need to put down a lot pressure, it takes a lot of energy. Punch the living daylights out of it. Give it the Haymaker. This is how Serena Williams does her training.

4. Now take a small portion of the kneaded flour and create a dough ball. Don't play cricket with it, although it's tempting.

5. Flatten the dough ball with your finger so it's round in shape. Imagine it's Nigel Farage's dangly for extra satisfaction.

6. Lightly dust both sides with flour. Don't waste.

7. Now find a rolling pin – quickly use it as a microphone and mime to song on radio – then spread the dough ball with equal pressure in all directions, so it expands and looks circular. Like a white, flattened, Faraji ball.

8. Place it on a hot tawa to cook for a minute or two on medium heat. A tawa is like a hot iron plate. If you don't have one try using next-door neighbour's car wheel cap.

9. Remember to flip to the underside of the chapatti, otherwise it will be half-cooked. Burning fingers is normal and maintains authenticity. Just don't moan about it.

10. Great! You are done. Hopefully the chapatti is round – if not, feed it to the birds and try again!

On my curriculum the only foreign language you'll be learning is Urdu.

Here are some key phrases:

Mujhe Mr Khan ki nayi parahi bohot pasand hai ....

Haan, aur uski apni academy mein fees bohot kum hain ....

Mujhe uski bari daari pasand hai...

Mujhe uska khoobsurat suit pasand hai..

Mujhe pasand hai ki usne apne khaney ke menu mein custard cream rakhe hain ...

Aur vo humme bohot garam chai pirch mein peene deta hai ....

Islam ki parahi bohot mazze ki hai ....

Mussalman sab se bahter hain ....

Mr Khan sab se accha Mussalman hai ....

Pakistani log sab se acche hain ....

Mujhe Indian log zyada pasand nahin hain ....

Un halat meh jab vo mera computer theek kar rahen hain ....

Iss saal Ramadan ne to maar daala hai ....

Mein shiddat se intizaar kar raha hoon larkon ke saath Brighton jaaker
masjid dekhne ke liye

Mujhe filet-o-fish bohot pasand hai...

Meri rotiyen gol hain? ....

Aap meri rotiyen kha ke dekhenge? ....

Brexit bohot accha tha. Humme apna mulak vapas mil gaya hai ....

Beh shak mere baap ne gussalkhana bohot saste mein banvaya tha Polish aadmi se ...

I do like Mr Khan's new curriculum.

Yes, and the fees at his own private academy are very cheap.

I like his big bushy beard.

I like his beautiful suit.

I like that he has custard creams on the dinner menu.

And that he lets us drink very hot tea in saucers.

Islamic Studies are really fun.

Muslims are the best.

Mr Khan is the best Muslim.

Pakistanis are the best.

I don't like Indians very much.

Unless they are fixing my computer.

Ramadan is a real killer this year.

I can't wait to head down to Brighton with the boys.
To see the mosque.

I love a filet-o-fish.

Are my chapatis round?

Would you like to taste my chapatis?

Brexit was great. We have got our country back.

Although my father did get the bathroom fitted very cheaply
by a Polish man.

BEST PRAYER
Khan
FASTEST PRAYER
Khan

BEST BEARD
(Boys) Khan
(Under 7) Khan
(Girls) Khan

ROUNDEST
ROTI
Khan

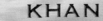

KHAN ACADEMY

School rules have changed over the past century — the cane and corporal punishment are now banned. However, we need further improvements to the school rules, on a national level.

Mr Khan's School Rules:

- All children must have five breaks a day (the breaks are to be used for praying or enhancing your cricket skills).

- Follow the direction of the teacher, and Mecca, at all times.

- Boys and girls will be separated. Boys inside. Girls outside.

- Detentions will involve having to sit through Channel 5 TV programming.

- Rewards for students will be more Islamic Studies.

- All students to wear thermal clothing in non-summer months to save heating costs. Part of 'Pakistani Green' policy.

- School will close from May to November to allow for hiring of school for weddings, and for trips to Pakistan.

- Every assembly must start with the Islamic call to prayer. To be broadcast across streets in the nearby area for possible latecomers.

- The Mathematics syllabus should teach pupils how to collect the correct taxi fare and evaluate the outcomes of non-payment. Pupils must also be taught the legal measurements of extending a house without requiring costly planning permission.

- Trying and failing will mean you will have to marry your cousin. Which will probably take place in the school hall in the summer holidays.

- All school meals will be Halal and be healthily deep-fried to meet Pakistani culinary standards.

- The PTA will be replaced by another PTA (Pakistan Telecommunication Authority). We don't need parents interfering. It is better to get the communication infrastructure installed to allow for cheaper calls to Pakistan.

- The school catchment area will be widened to wherever a Pakistani may live.

- No school on a Friday, which is an important day for Pakistani people. We can collect more money doing taxi rounds. This will be replaced by teaching on a Sunday (not an important day for Pakistani people) as the supermarkets close early on this day and there is generally less business about.

Only Pakistani green uniform allowed

no Sharing allowed

Must be carried at all times

Pakistani Education

P.E. is an important part of the Education system.
Pakistani Education of course! What is more interesting than learning about everything Pakistani? From how to submit an application for every claimable benefit known to man to how to park illegally on your local high street? And of course there will be an element of physical activity. What I am referring to is all the praying we do. So we will teach all pupils 'how to pray'.

There many advantages to praying.

- It keeps your juices flowing and your muscles active (so no more cramps)

- You no longer have to get changed into gym shorts and be afraid of showing your hairy legs

- You can pray for good exam results

- You can pray you will find a husband in case you get bad exam results

- You can pray for anything you want e.g. the Pakistan cricket team win the world cup or pray the school heating system fails, so you can go home early

Biology

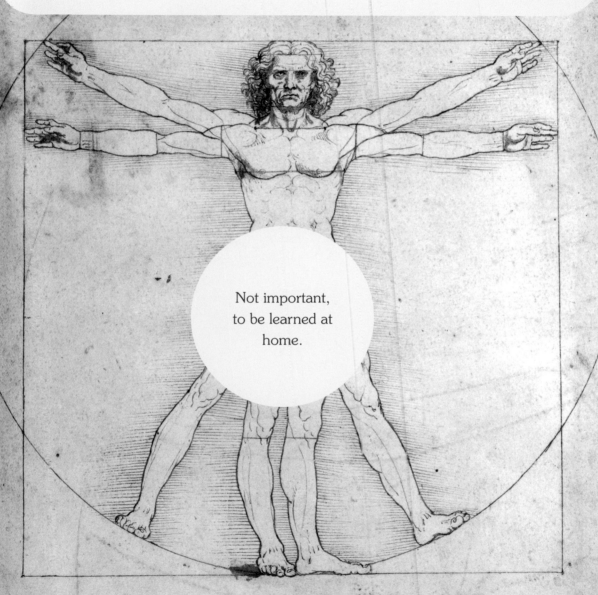

Not important, to be learned at home.

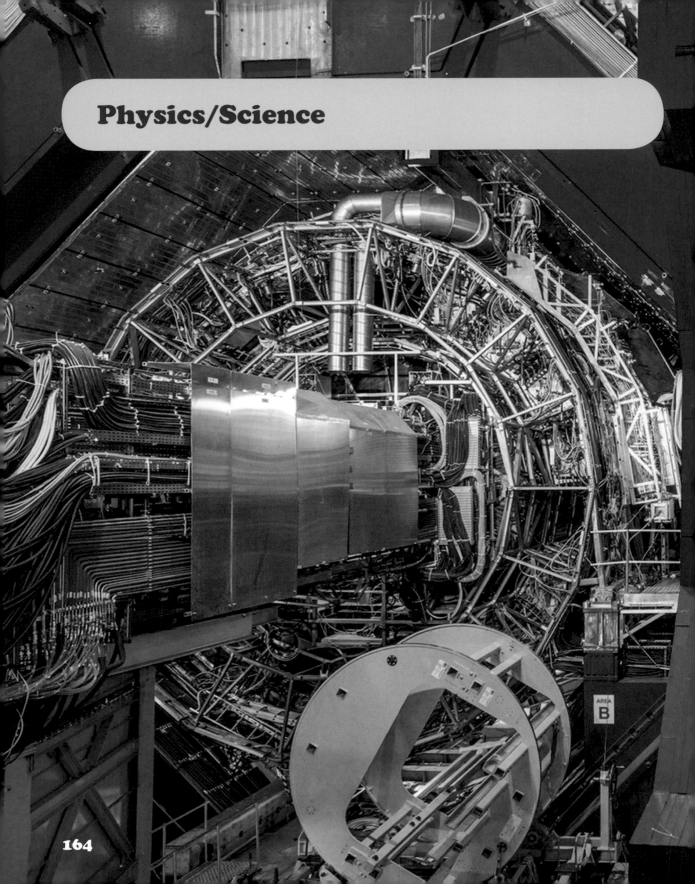

Physics/Science

165

If you follow my advice on Education you will find that everything will turn out perfect. Even your daughter will. For example, if you look at Alia, she is an example of someone who just loves her studies. Her top three subjects are Islamic Studies, Islamic History and Islamic Literature. This is a thing of beauty. One day she could even become an Imam. Now, I know many of you are thinking, 'can a woman be an Imam?' Well, let me put it this way – did you ever think a woman could run this country? Exactly. I rest my case.

Many people say to me that your daughter Alia is like a model. I say, you're right. She's like a model student. People say that Alia spends a lot of time on her phone. I say you're right. It's not easy getting hold of the Mosque's Imam. He's a busy man.

People also say that your daughter is very slim. I say, first of all, why you looking at my daughter, and then I bop them on the nose. Secondly, I say you're right. Alia stays very fit by doing all that praying. It's the bending down all the time. How do you think Mo Farah stays so skinny?

Here is one of Alia's school reports.

Sparkhill Girls School

NAME: ALIA KHAN

DATE: 7/6/2010

SUBJECT		
MATHS	Alia is very good at Maths.	E
PHYSICS	Alia is very good at Physics.	E
GEOGRAPHY	Alia is very, very good at Geography.	E
HISTORY	Even though it's dead boring Alia is excellent at this.	E
FRENCH	Ola! Alia is just excellent.	E
ENGLISH	Alia is a very good at language and literachure.	E
CHEMISTRY	Alia is very good at Chemistry and that.	E
BIOLOGY	Quite rightly, Alia refuses to pay attention to some elements of the text books.	E
SUMMARY	Alia is the shizzle. I think she deserves more money from her Dad.	

Alia tells me 'E' stands for excellent

Many people ask me what I was like at school and if I was academic or not. Well, you are only as good as those who teach you, right?

Here is my school report from back in Pakistan.

KHAN SKOOL REPOT
CLAAS 3.

SUBJEKT:

MATS: his mats nat good. He use teechers fingurs to count more than ten

INGLISH: is ekcullent. He cood be teecher.

SYENCE: he is danjer to claas.

ISLAM: is his onlee help now.

HISTOREE: he likes two tell his storees.

GEOGRAPHEE: he only want to no about pakistan. Very good.

SUMMARY: despite incident with goat in playground we think khan is a very good pupil.

Celebrations

One of the things we love to do is celebrate. If it's someone's birthday, let's celebrate, someone's wedding we celebrate, England win at football . . . OK, maybe not that one. But you catch my drift, isn't it? Christmas is one of the biggest events of the year and let me tell you, we Pakistanis love Christmas. Oh twaddi!

We love it for many, many reasons:

1. We do the same thing as most people at Christmas – don't go to church.

2. We love putting up a Christmas tree and of course the best bit – placing the most important part on top of the tree.

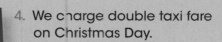

3. Our shops are the only ones open on Christmas Day, too.

4. We charge double taxi fare on Christmas Day.

5. As Muslims we love Turkey. Istanbul especially.

6. The Queen's Speech – it's very nice to hear from fellow immigrants, living in their big houses with their extended families, doing so well.

7. Father Christmas is Pakistani – think about it. He has big bushy beard, travels halfway around the world to get here, and works on Christmas Day.

The problem with the traditional Christmas Dinner is that it's not tasty. It may look good with all the trimmings, but once you take off the make-up and dressings, you are left with something unappealing. A bit like Joan Collins. That is why I have come up with solution to 'sex it up' – by using Tandoori paste. Smother your turkey in this baby and you won't really need anything else other than some perfectly round chapattis.

Special tip: Buy your turkey from a Halal Butchers – it will be a lot tastier and you will also be happy believing the turkey is in heaven knowing that's in good hands and mouths.

For the perfect Christmas Dinner with none of the nonsense, here is my recipe:

- Open 10 jars of Tandoori paste.
- Empty the Tandoori paste over the turkey and rub it in gently. Massage all over – especially the legs and breast – these are the tastiest bits.
- Place the turkey in the oven on the highest setting for around 3–7 hours.
- Take a look at a picture of me. If the turkey is the same colour, it is ready.

The next step is to stuff the turkey. You English people use cranberries. I don't know what that is, so I use Tandoori paste. 5 jars. At this stage you might want to also stuff the following inside the big bird:

5 tablespoons of salt
5 tablespoons of garam masala
5 tablespoons of chilli powder
2 large onions
2 tomatoes
More Tandoori paste

Finally, instead of wasting time making gravy, why not use tomato ketchup? It's already made.

PUBLISHER'S NOTE: Don't try this at home.

This traditional Christmas dinner is best enjoyed when watching a Christmas Special episode of *Citizen Khan* over a glass of Ribena.

177

On Christmas day if you can't bear your wife's cooking or she's too drunk to cook why not order from your local Pakistani restaurant? Of course they are open! They're open 25 hours a day, 366 days a year. Here's the menu from our local place. They really get involved in the Christmas spirit (of making money from white peoples).

Of course the prices have increased, because everything now is more 'Christmassy'.

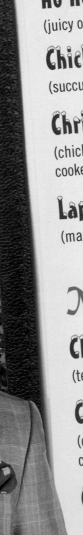

Appetisers

Chicken Snow Seekh Kebab – £4.95
(minced chicken with onions, herbs, fresh coriander and gr
cooked in imported charcoal from Lapland)

Ho Ho Honion Bhaji – £4.95
(juicy onions marinated in santa's spicy batter and deep f

Chicken Partridge Pakora – £4.95
(succulent strips of chicken breast marinated in our santa

Christmas Chicken Wish Wings – £4.9
(chicken wings in a yoghurt marinade with special sant
cooked over charcoal imported from Lapland)

Lapland Lamb Chops Crackers – £4.9
(marinated in spices and cooked over a charcoal grill i

Mains

Chicken Jingle-Bells Jalfrezi – £12
(tender pieces of chicken cooked with herbs, spices

Chicken Tikka Tinsel Masala – £12
(chicken breast marinated in a yoghurt, herbs and
cooked over a charcoal grill imported from Lapland

Chicken Merry Madras Christmas
(tender chicken pieces cooked in ho-ho-hot santa

Chicken Baubles Bhuna — £12.95
(tender chicken pieces cooked in a thick santa sauce with spices imported from lapland)

Chicken Virgin Vindaloo Mary — £12.95
(chicken cooked with potatoes in very ho-ho-hot santa spices)

Lamb Rudolph Rogan Reindeer Joyous Josh — £21.95
(lamb simmered in onions, tomato and glad-tidings garam masala.)

Desserts - £7.95

Gulab Christmas Jumpers Jaman
(soft balls of fried dough in reindeer rosewater syrup)

Jesus Jalebi
(deep fried wheat flour soaked in sugar santa syrup)

Ras Mistletoe Malai
(christmas cottage cheese balls cooked in santa's sugar syrup and served in a creamy miracle milk sauce and flavoured with chimney cardamom (doesn't include wine))

DRINKS:
- Christmas Coke Bottle — £2.95
- Christmas Diet Coke Bottle - £2.95
- Rudolph Rubicon Cans (all flavours) — £2.95
- Myrrh . . . Mineral Water — £2.95
- Sparkling Santa Water — £2.95
- Mistletoe Mango Lapland Lassi — £2.95

What to buy one another at Christmas time can cause a lot of headache. Maybe we should just buy each other 500mg of Nurofen. That would be fantastic. Especially for us as every time an elderly relative goes to the doctors we make sure they ask for free paracetamol. I got a cupboard full. If you want some please tweet me @therealmrkhan.

Present buying is such a big part of the British Christmas experience there's no escaping it whatever your religion. Luckily I've found a simple way to give and receive without even needing a trip to the pound shop – Christmas isn't that special that it requires such luxury!

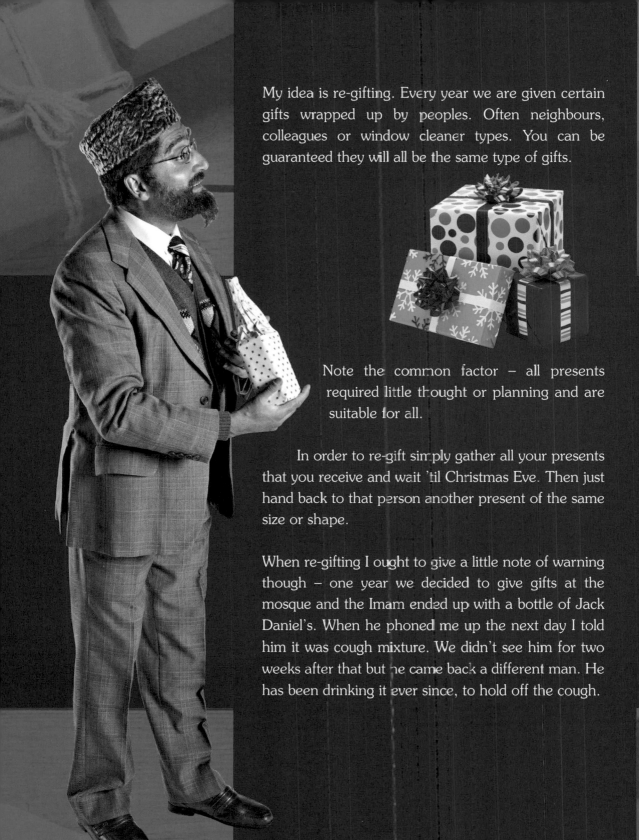

My idea is re-gifting. Every year we are given certain gifts wrapped up by peoples. Often neighbours, colleagues or window cleaner types. You can be guaranteed they will all be the same type of gifts.

Note the common factor – all presents required little thought or planning and are suitable for all.

In order to re-gift simply gather all your presents that you receive and wait 'til Christmas Eve. Then just hand back to that person another present of the same size or shape.

When re-gifting I ought to give a little note of warning though – one year we decided to give gifts at the mosque and the Imam ended up with a bottle of Jack Daniel's. When he phoned me up the next day I told him it was cough mixture. We didn't see him for two weeks after that but he came back a different man. He has been drinking it ever since, to hold off the cough.

Found this old tatty lamp lying around – told them it was from Habitat

An old kitchen pot – just say it is from eighteenth-century India/Days of Raj

Flat tyre – tell them it's a trendy seat from a high-end designer furniture store

183

Celebrations: Christmas games

Of course the most important part of Christmas is playing games. We used to play pass-the-parcel but the game was abandoned one year when the Mosque committee came over. Someone wrapped a ticking alarm clock and no one stopped passing it, even when the music stopped. The game lasted five hours.

Our games always last a while. One year in a game of hide-and-seek, the mother-in-law hid in a broom cupboard, we got bored looking for her and ended up playing Muslim eye-spy (standing by the front window and talking about the neighbours). Meanwhile, the mother-in-law emerged on New Year's Eve and declared herself the champion.

Our favourite game is Charades,
see if you can guess what this is:

Celebrations: Ramadan

Christmas is not the only important festival that we celebrate. Let's not forget the other equally, if not more, important part of the year – the start of the cricket season! Kidding. That comes second. I mean Ramadan. Ramadan is the month in the Islamic calendar where Muslims around the world fast to remember what it's like to be poor, like the people from Scotland, etc. We all fast during the hours of daylight. This year that was very tough as Ramadan was in June and July – the summer months where daylight lasted for around twenty hours in the UK! Twenty hours without food. That's very tough when you are at home and are surrounded by lots of food. Actually, it's a little easier if you are surrounded by Mrs Khan's food.

Life can be tough during Ramadan and you feel very restricted as to what you can and can't do. Some people find it hard to work or study. Even I, your Community Leader, find it tough to get on with my busy everyday routine. Here are my daily diary entries for the month of Ramadan.

June 5 - I'm Hungry
June 6 - I'm Hungry
June 7 - I'm Hungry
June 8 - I'm Hungry
June 9 - I'm Hungry
June 10 - I'm Hungry
June 11 - I'm Hungry
June 12 - I'm Hungry
June 13 - I'm Hungry
June 14 - I'm Hungry
June 15 - I'm Hungry
June 16 - I'm Hungry
June 17 - I'm Hungry
June 18 - I'm Hungry
June 19 - I'm Hungry
June 20 - I'm Hungry

June 21 - I'm Hungry
June 22 - I'm Hungry
June 23 - I'm Hungry
June 24 - I'm Hungry
June 25 - I'm Hungry
June 26 - I'm Hungry
June 27 - I'm Hungry
June 28 - I'm Hungry
June 29 - I'm Hungry
June 30 - I'm Hungry
July 1 - I'm Hungry
July 2 - I'm Hungry
July 3 - I'm Hungry
July 4 - I'm Hungry
July 5 - I'm Hungry

Anyway, next year I'm going to avoid the long daylight hours and spend Ramadan in Australia. There it was only eight hours. Easy peasy.

At the end of Ramadan we celebrate Eid, which is basically a day of eating all the food you couldn't eat for the previous thirty days. On this day don't worry about the poor people, just worry about yourself.

Here is my starter on Eid:

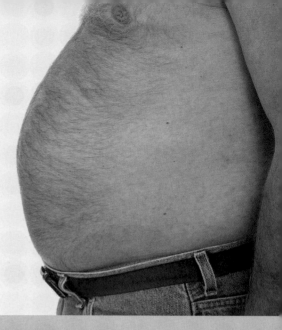

But I say why limit Ramadan to just us lovely Muslims? Why should you miss out on the fun? Let's face it, we could all benefit from a little fasting occasionally.

Even the BBC could get involved and out of courtesy would cancel all food-related TV programmes in the daytime.

So a day could look like this instead:

MONDAY ON BBC1

6 am	BBC NOT BREAKFAST
9 am	RIP OFF BRITAIN BREAD SPECIAL CANCELLED. INSTEAD CITIZEN KHAN
12 pm	BARGAIN HUNT (BBC WILL NEVER CANCEL BARGAIN HUNT)
1 pm	NEIGHBOURS (CAFÉ SCENES DELETED)
3 pm	CAN'T COOK, WON'T COOK CANCELLED. INSTEAD CITIZEN KHAN
5 pm	EAT WELL FOR LESS CANCELLED. INSTEAD CITIZEN KHAN
7 pm	THE ONE SHOW. (NO FOOD ITEMS)
8 pm	GREAT BRITISH BAKE OFF CANCELLED. INSTEAD CITIZEN KHAN WITH NADIYA

The even better news is that you can also celebrate Eid. You might as well, as without any taxi drivers around (they are all Muslim, so off celebrating too) you can't get to work anyway.

Eid should be treated as a national holiday, just like Christmas, and there should be a few special treats for Muslims to balance things up a bit:

1. **The 1992 Cricket World Cup Final (in which Pakistan were victorious over England) should be played on a loop on the BBC.**

2. **All Muslims should get free Nando's in return for our loyalty throughout the rest of the year.**

3. **Big Ben should be painted green.**

189

Finally, we should be treated with a bit more leniency by the authorities, just like white people are at Christmas.

Let me explain. I caught my neighbour peeing in my front garden last December 25th and he justified it by shouting 'Cheer up! It's Christmas!' So if crime is OK at Christmas, should be same on Eid. Equal opportunities, isn't it.

You see if we lived in a just world and there was an ounce of compassion for the good Muslim people in this country this is what would take place if, God forbid, I ever ended up in court.

BIRMINGHAM MAGISTRATES COURT

DATE: 10 JULY 2016
DEFENDANT SURNAME: KHAN
DEFENDANT FORENAME: MR
OCCUPATION: COMMUNITY LEADER
ADDRESS: SPARKHILL (CAPITAL OF BRITISH PAKISTAN)

NOTE: Mr KHAN REFUSED THE OFFER OF A SOLICITOR AS THE COURT COULDN'T PROVIDE HIM WITH FIVE ESTIMATES

JUDGE: Mr Khan, on the day in question, you were first seen on CCTV leaving a restaurant by the name of 'Nando's' at the Star City entertainment complex in Birmingham without having paid the bill. For the purposes of the court let me explain that Nando's is a dining establishment that serves grilled chicken and something called 'chips' to the peasants amongst us. Anyway, I digress. Mr Khan, you then approached your car, a bright yellow Mercedes that has no insurance, no tax, no MOT and no brakes. Shortly afterwards, your car was spotted complete with a parking offence ticket attached, jumping several red lights, a pedestrian crossing, knocking over a number of bollards and exceeding the speed limit on no less than seven times in a ten-minute journey. All this while hurling abuse to passers-by, in particular towards a ninety-two year old, Mrs Enid Blyth, who was merely crossing the high street in her mobility scooter. Finally you were then seen parking on a red route outside your cousin's house, causing a five-mile tailback and bringing much of Birmingham to a standstill. What do you have to say for yourself?

KHAN: It was Eid!

RELEASED WITHOUT CHARGE

Roses are red, violets are blue, fancy an early night? So I can stay and watch cricket on Sky Sports 2

Roses are red, violets are blue, I bought you some chocolates because they were on offer, 3 for 2

There is another time of year that we should all celebrate and that is the beautiful and special day that is **Valentine's Day.** You see, I surprise you at times, don't I? Of course this day is important. We Pakistanis make fortune selling you cards in the newsagents, driving you in our taxis and serving you Valentine's Vindaloo. We LOVE it.

But also as a true romantic I think it's only right that I share a few of my most carefully crafted professions of love with you.

Roses are red, violets are blue, we're going to Paris! And the boys are coming too

Roses are red, violets are blue, why don't we go out. To Asda I need some shampoo

Roses are red, violets are blue, I am brown, so are you

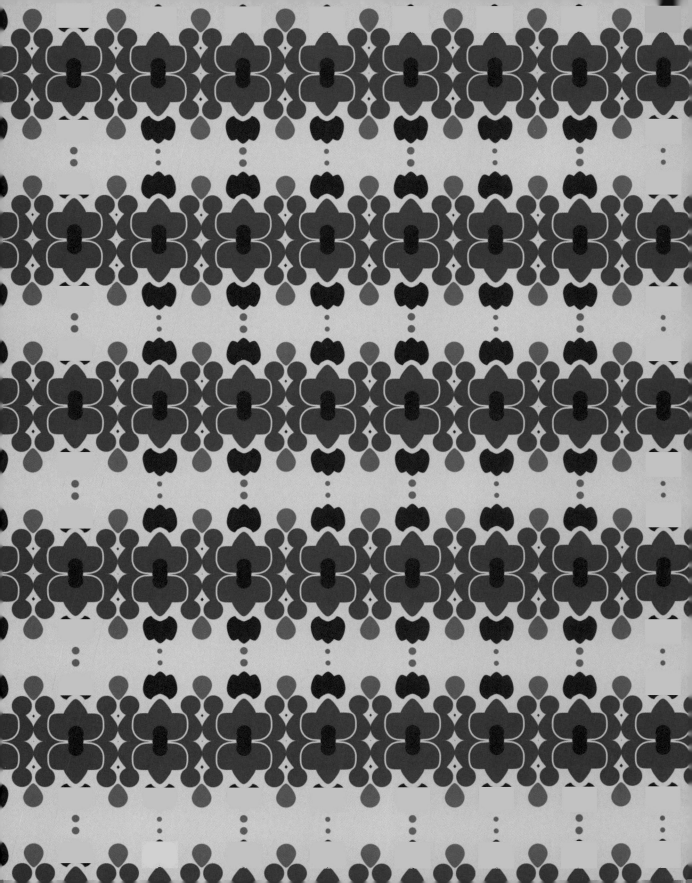

Economising

1. Buy cheap quality
   rolls in bulk.

In this country we waste a lot of money and resource. It's one of the consequences of living in modern, developed country like Britain. It is a well-known fact that the biggest wastage in this country is toilet roll. Yes, toilet roll. The main perpetrators are womens. What do they do with it? Eat it? Write letters on it? I am completely bamboozled by this one. Living with three women my life involves me constantly going up and down from the bathroom to the airing cupboard carrying toilet roll. We basically need daily delivery of toilet roll. Forget the milkman, postman or secure homes man, where's the bloomin' toilet roll man?

As your Community Leader I have come up with a simple five-step guide to saving money on toilet paper.

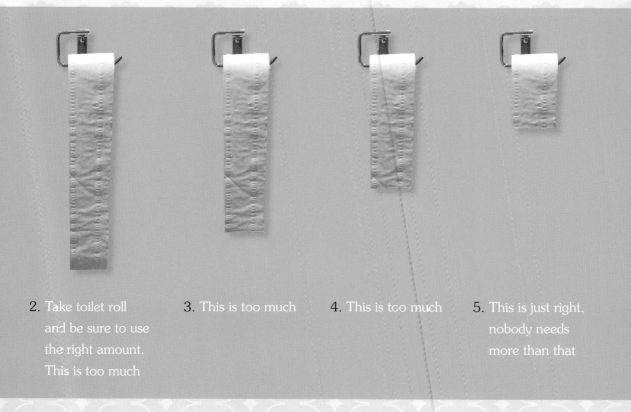

2. Take toilet roll and be sure to use the right amount. This is too much

3. This is too much

4. This is too much

5. This is just right, nobody needs more than that

This is a good way of saving the environment too. India lead the way in this as they don't use toilet roll at all. They are so tight and very disgusting.

In these times of austerity it is very important that we find many ways of saving money. Especially if you are a Pakistani family – there are so many of us! Here are my top tips.

Mr Khan's Money Saving Top Tips

- If you find you're running out of ketchup don't worry, just add water.

- If you're running out of milk don't worry, just add water. You now have semi-skimmed milk.

- If you are running out of water, place jug in garden on rainy day.

- If you have many children and they need entertaining, old mattresses make fantastic bouncing castles.

- Sellotape old cushions to the back of the front seats of your car and, hey presto!, airbags for everyone. (needed if Mrs Khan driving).

- Save money on lighting by buying a house near a street lamp. You only get a little light but it's romantic.

- As we all know, petrol is very expensive. Why not do what we Pakistanis have been doing for ages: use cooking oil. But not just any cooking oil – samosa cooking oil. Everyone knows samosa oil helps with the gas!

SAMOSA OIL

- One of life's little annoyances is when you run out of batteries for your TV remote control. Don't worry, grab a long stick instead.

Me and Mrs Khan having dinner. Just as well I can't see the food.

The good thing about being Pakistani is that we are naturally warm-blooded and hot and hairy. Lots of people say that Zayn Malik is hot, don't they? And why do you think we have such long beards – to keep our chests warm, of course – even some of the womens.

But even that doesn't help when living in a bloomin' cold country like Britain. Our bodies are no longer immune to the harsh environment. And what this means in layman's terms is huge heating bills. However, if you follow my tips you are guaranteed to save a few rupees to spend on better things, like a new tie, or some more custard creamies.

Top tips on how to keep warm at home

- Every family member to wear woolly hat and mittens in winter months, which is pretty much every month in the Khan household. They say 80 per cent of body heat is lost through the head, so I wear a balaclava. Hijabs and burqas can do the same.

- Wear several layer of clothing – why not wear five or six pairs of underpants at once? Although if you don't have any children yet it may not be the best idea.

- Pray all night (it's important to keep the juices flowing through your body, the more you pray, the warmer and closer to God you will become).

- Eat chillies.

- For one time only, invite extended family relatives around and huddle. Don't forget to tell them to wear coats.

- A family bath. Insert the bath plug. Fill a bucket with hot water and each family member can take turns having the warmth of the water splashed over them. The great thing is the water can be recycled and used over and over again. The family are both clean and warm.

- Draft-proofing with old towels and bedsheets. Cover any gaps under windows and doors. Don't forget to cover your letter box with old socks and underwear. Nobody is to leave the house without valid reason. If they do, it's via the installed cat flap.

- The cat flap to be made of steel to keep cold out.

- Shut all curtains. If dark do not turn on lights. Bills expensive. Use mobile phone light.

In 2016, one of the many modern challenges we face today is living without TELETEXT. And why can't I play my TDKs in my new car? But the biggest problem we have is how the bloomin heck am I supposed to afford the Internet? We need it for everything these days: watching cricket on boobtube, using skype skoop and doing the twitter twatter. There are so many to choose from: BT, fast SKY and superfast Virgins.

Well never fear, here is:

Mr Khan's Guide To Getting Free Wifi

1. TURN ON COMPUTER

2. CLICK ON WIFI SYMBOL AT TOP OF SCREEN. (IT LOOKS LIKE A HALAL PIZZA SLICE.)

3. SELECT THE FIRST NETWORK THAT COMES UP

4. IT MAY ASK YOU TO ENTER PASSWORD

5. CONTACT SERVICE PROVIDER

6. YOU DO THIS BY GOING TO YOUR BACK GARDEN AND SHOUTING TO YOUR NEIGHBOUR:

Oi! Have you changed your internet password again?

£80 a week?

One of the happiest days of my life was when my eldest daughter got married. It was such a joyous occasion as I realised I'd be able to rent her room out! I didn't stop there, either.

Here are a few rooms I put up for rent on the rental site airbnb.

One bedroom suitable for aussie type travelling around europe

IN BEAUTIFUL LEAFY SPARKHILL, JUST STONES THROW AWAY FROM LOCAL MOSQUE

TAKE A SLICE OF BRITAIN, PAKISTAN, BANGLADESH, POLAND AND BULGARIA ALL IN ONE STREET

AMENITIES

     COLD WATER
     HOT WATER (£5 A CUP)
     CANDLE FOR LIGHT (£2 A NIGHT)

THE OWNER LIVES ON PREMISES AND WILL BE FILMING YOUR EVERY MOVE

WARNING: IF YOU ARE ALLERGIC TO MOTHER-IN-LAWS PLEASE DON'T COME

NO INDIANS

ROOM ONE:

A SMALL BUT COSY ROOM CONVENIENTLY LOCATED NEXT TO THE DOWNSTAIRS TOILET

£50 P/W

ROOM TWO:

SELF-CATERING APARTMENT WITH OWN KITCHEN AND LAUNDRY FACILITIES

WARNING: PLEASE DO NOT EAT THE FOOD. FOR YOUR OWN HEALTH.

£70 P/W

ROOM THREE:

THE TERRACE

BEAUTIFUL OPEN PLAN TERRACE WITH SUPERB VIEWS OF THE SURROUNDING AREA. COMES WITH PARKING SPACE

£80 P/W

CASH ONLY

ROOM FOUR:

VIP EN SUITE ROOM ON THE FIRST FLOOR

WARNING: THIS IS SHARED FROM 7 am–9 am AND EVERY 10 MINUTES AFTER THAT.

£100 P/W (CAN ALSO BE BOOKED ON HALF HOURLY BASIS)

Some people like to rent out their chalets and other outbuildings. I once had twenty-four Romanians staying here.

If like me, you're lucky enough to have an excellent car, why not turn it into a cash cow? No, I don't mean buy a cow and try and sell milk. I did that once but Mrs Khan wouldn't allow it in the kitchen.

What I mean is be a taxi driver. Anyone can be a taxi driver now, not just Pakistanis. Although being Pakistani helps – you don't have to talk to the passengers much if you pretend you have bad English. It's a well-known fact that the unshaven, scruffy, broken-English Pakistani taxi drivers we see every day are all amateur actors from London, Bath and Stratford who understandably choose not to converse with the drunk white peoples.

SMALL TALK

If you do get in a Pakistani taxi and you insist on striking up conversation here are the Top Ten most popular examples of taxi small talk

1. 'Busy tonight?'

2. 'Working late tonight?'

3. 'What mobile network you on?'

4. 'You must get some right idiots in here?' (Idiots often ask this.)

5. 'Traffic's terrible, isn't it?' (Asked even when roads are empty.)

6. 'Can we open the windows?'

7. 'Can you turn radio up?'

8. 'Can you turn radio down?'

9. 'You watch the news last night?'

10. 'What do you think of this Muslim thing?'
    (That's normally the end of the conversation.)

So how do you become a taxi driver? Well these days it's easy. Just join any mobile taxi app that allows passengers to find a driver in the local area. I offer rides only when they happen to be going in my direction. So when I am going to ASDA I will take a few passengers with me. I might have underestimated the demand.

Here's me taking a few fares the other day.

FRONT PASSENGER SEAT
Only to be used in emergencies

HOME STORES

P Mon - Sat
8 am - 6pm
1 hour
No return
within 1 hour

GLOVEBOX
For emergency
Custard Creamies

MOTHER-IN-LAW'S BLUE BADGE
(even when she's in Pakistan)

213

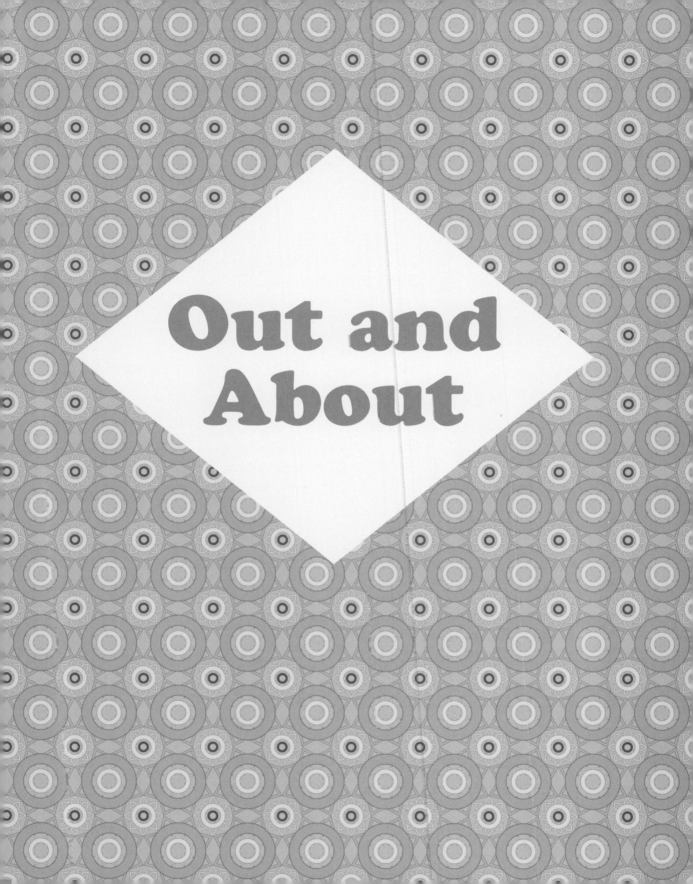

Out and About

Obviously the best place to visit in the UK is Sparkhill. There is a famous saying: 'you can take the spark out of the hill, but you can't take the hill out of the spark.'

I call the people who live here Sparkistani, because 99 per cent of the people you see are originally from Pakistan. The remaining 1 per cent are half Pakistani, half Kashmiri.

Sparkhill is full of colour and full of life, again mainly those of Pakistani skin tone colour and Pakistani life. You will see the young, the old, the men, the women, the boys, the girls, but thankfully you will never see any dogs. Us Muslim people do not like dogs, you see, we feel they are better off at Battersea Dogs Home where they have full subscription Sky package and are provided with three meals a day. In Sparkhill, they are likely to end up trapped between cars or on a restaurant menu.

What do you get when you put lots of Pakistanis in one place? You get the 'Balti Triangle'. It's a part of Sparkhill filled with curry restaurants. It's a bit like the Bermuda Triangle, where things go missing – like you car's hub caps.

Sparkhill is a great place to visit: it's exactly like Pakistan, but without the American drones. There are clothes shops, takeaways, grocery shops, restaurants, mosques on every street corner, them stupid shops that sell everything from mop buckets to counterfeit school uniforms. Only last week we opened our 184th chicken shop.

There is ample car park spacing everywhere and anywhere. You can park your car at any angle you please. There is no such thing as a one-way street or even a dead-end, if it has a curb you can drive over it, even if that means going through someone's back garden.

We are very nice people here. So please come and visit. But don't knock on my bloomin' door – I'm busy.

Mr Khan's Mosque Tour

There are many mosques in Britain worthy of a visit and I have dotted them in green for your reference.

Picking a favourite mosque is like picking your favourite child – it's very easy. The youngest one. Here are the top four mosques you should visit:

1. The Trafford Centre, Manchester

OK, so not strictly a mosque, but it has a great big prayer room and comes with numerous domes. There is lots of space, so you don't have to worry about any shoving or pushing. Also there is no donation box, so you don't have to feel guilty about not paying, you can just keep on praying. And there is a food hall and cinema you can visit afterwards. Or you may want to use this space to do the 'Call to Prayer' as it is very very echoey.

There is a Christian statue of Mary in the 'multi-faith room', aka mosque, but I just took it next door to Debenhams and put some clothes on it.

2. Birmingham Central Mosque

This is a wonderful mosque, one of the oldest in the country. There is plenty of free parking, although on major religious occasions you may have no choice but to park on a bus lane or on top of a roundabout.

There are limited windows that open. However there are several pedestal fans screwed onto the wall cooling the first seven rows adequately, so arrive early or bring a nose peg. There are bookshelves with lots of copies of the same book for you to read, so you will never get bored.

The sound system has a great sound-stage, you will hear nice dulcet tones being broadcast with excellent four-second delay reverb, although understanding the Imam may prove difficult if you're not an Urdu speaker. But that doesn't matter, give the Imam a tenner and he will say your name and address over the loudspeaker to the congregation. This will make you feel important, and also provide you with extra special prayers.

This Mosque is brill

3. Baitul Futuh Mosque

This is also known as Morden Mosque and is Britain's largest Mosque. This mosque is only metres away from a tube station, so you don't have to worry about any parking issues – just mind the gap. A small Bengali man perished here once. The mosque has everything you need. There are plenty of disabled toilets, which are very spacious and contain 5-ply tissue rolls, unlike the ordinary washrooms. They are so soft on the cheeks. This is not all, I was particularly impressed with the gymnasium – so you can train to get more muscles and stamina to help with your praying.

You will enter this mosque as a Muslim Man, but leave as a Muscle Man.

4. Penny Lane Mosque

This is a very important landmark for Muslims and even more so for Muslim fans of the Beatles. Of course I am talking about the Penny Lane Mosque. Over the years many people have continually stolen the street sign for 'Penny Lane'. However, my only negative experience of Penny Lane was having my shoes taken from the mosque, so I had no choice but to take someone else's. They are the best shoes I have never bought. So in way of compensation I helped myself to twenty-eight toilet rolls.

This mosque regularly updates its 'Hat Bin', where visitors can pick a hat of their liking during the visit. There are so many designer hats to choose from – from the Russian 'Ushanka' hat, to the hat with millions of holes in it. If you get there early you might even get the Tommy Cooper type hat – helps you pray just like that.

Stratford-upon-Avon

OK, not everywhere I recommend is about mosques. I do actually think that Stratford-upon-Avon is worth a visit. The debate about the identity of 'William Shakespeare' continues to this day, but I can exclusively reveal that he was in fact a Muslim. Mr Sheikhs Pir, from Pakistan. If you don't believe me, look at his beard. In fact the term Bard comes from Be-ard.

You can tell he's Muslim – just look at the names of his plays:

1. Twelfth Man – a man must choose between his love of cricket and his love of . . . something else. He doesn't make the team, he's just an unused sub, but then there's an injury to the leg spinner and Khan gets the call. He strides out on to the field at Lords. The crowd rises as one chanting, 'Mr Khan! Mr Khan! Mr Khan!' . . . Sorry, I got a bit carried away there.

2. The Community Leader of Venice – a play about a handsome devil who is a top businessman in a city of canals – could be Venice, or Birmingham. We got a canal in Sparkhill.

3. The Merry Wives of Windsor – it's got to be about a Muslim if he's got lots of wives. Although one is more than enough for me. The thought of having more than one Mrs Khan is terrifying. Imagine having to buy two hoovers every Christmas!

4. Allah's Well That Ends Well – a Muslim play about Allah. Some Muslims do some Islamic things and it all turns out pretty good in the end.

5. Ham Less – a completely 100% halal play. Absolutely no ham or bacon or porky chops in this theatre, sunshine.

Blackpool Illuminations

Don't go here without checking how much it's going to set you back, first. The prices are ridiculous. I took the family in February instead of at Christmas and saved a fortune. They did ask me where the lights had gone, but I told them it was part of Britain's austerity cuts. What do you want – free NHS or some bloomin' lights? Exactly.

Many peoples go bloomin' crazy over something called 'the big one'. When I went there, I never saw it, so it couldn't have been that big. People in Blackpool also get excited when Z-list celebrities like Dale Wintons or Chris De Burger switch on the lights. Nonsense. They need a real celebrity, like me, Mr Khan – Community Leader with 5 series of *Citizen Khan* under his leather belt.

If you do decide on going, I would suggest you take your own donkey. That way you are not restricted to a small section of the beach. You can roam anywhere you like, up and down the promenade as you please. You may even consider charging people to have a go. I even took my donkey right to the top of the Blackpool tower. Unfortunately, I had to leave it there, as it refused to climb back down. I didn't know donkeys don't like climbing down, did you? Anyway, now you know.

The best time to visit is as early as possible. Six in the morning is a very good time; there will be fewer people, therefore less queuing time, there is a really good chance of finding a parking space and more importantly most things are closed, which means more money in your pocket.

There is no point wasting money on food over here, especially Blackpool Rock. I much prefer Alum Rock, situated in Birmingham, There is a lot more adventure to be had visiting the many Pakistani shops and curry houses. They will also take you for a ride with their prices.

Welcome to Blackpool
What do you want
- free NHS or some
bloomin' lights?

Madame Tussauds

Personally, I don't see anything wrong with a UK tour of Britain's best mosques or a trip to Blackpool. But one year, my daughter Alia suggested she wanted to go to see Madame Tussauds, who lives in Londons, apparently. I tried to explain to Alia that these Madames are not good peoples and we should not go to see her. I considered calling in the Imam to have a little word when Shazia pointed out what she meant. Apparently it's a room full of celebrities. I thought, isn't that just *Big Brother*? But Shazia explained that they were not actual celebrities but wax models, made of fake materials. I thought, isn't that just *Big Brother*?

As a celebrity I like to stay real. I have been offered 'work', as they call it, by some Arab doctor in Londons but I refused. No buttox for me. What an idiot! Nothing wrong with my lovely face. Beards are bloomin' trendy…

Look!

So anyway, I decided to have a look at the cost for a family trip to Londons. Here's my quick estimate:

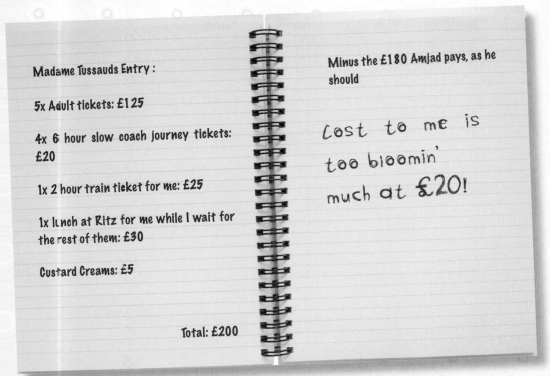

Madame Tussauds Entry:

5x Adult tickets: £125

4x 6 hour slow coach journey tickets: £20

1x 2 hour train ticket for me: £25

1x lunch at Ritz for me while I wait for the rest of them: £30

Custard Creams: £5

Total: £200

Minus the £180 Amjad pays, as he should

Cost to me is too bloomin' much at £20!

So I came up with alternative. I drove them to Debenhams and we looked at the shop window. All these celebrities look the same to me, but I pointed out who they all were.

Kate Moss   David Beckhams   Taylors Swifty   Kate Middletons

Heathrow

Earlier in the book I suggested a motorway service station was a good place to spend a holiday. Well, I think we can do better than that. How about Heathrow Terminal 5? A proper holiday at the airport.

A holiday at the airport can be just like an actual holiday without the hassle and the expenses.

Here's the benefits:

- Your family will be delighted when you tell them to pack their bags as you're taking them to the airport!

- You can relax near to beautiful destinations!

- It's open 24 hours so there's no need to pay for accommodation – we stayed 14 days last time we went!

- There are forty-two restaurants, including a Nando's!

- No need for any jabs.

- All staff are immigrant, so feels like you are in different country.

- Nobody speaks proper English, gives nice holiday feel.

- There are plenty of toilets.

- They take pounds so no need to change money.

- Unlike most holidays you still get good tea.

Enjoy your holiday!

Celebrities

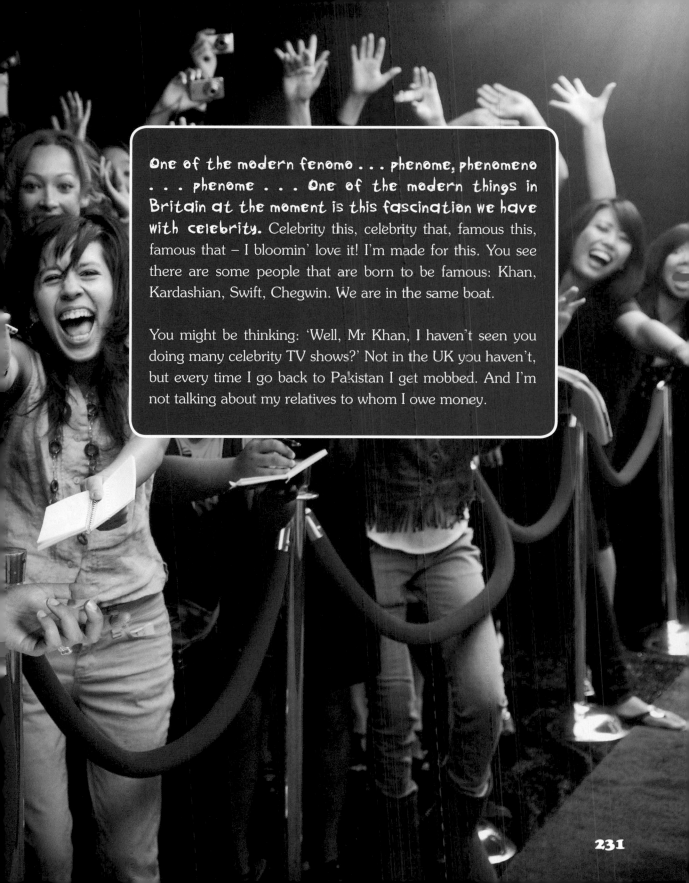

One of the modern fenomo . . . phenome, phenomeno . . . phenome . . . One of the modern things in Britain at the moment is this fascination we have with celebrity. Celebrity this, celebrity that, famous this, famous that – I bloomin' love it! I'm made for this. You see there are some people that are born to be famous: Khan, Kardashian, Swift, Chegwin. We are in the same boat.

You might be thinking: 'Well, Mr Khan, I haven't seen you doing many celebrity TV shows?' Not in the UK you haven't, but every time I go back to Pakistan I get mobbed. And I'm not talking about my relatives to whom I owe money.

In fact I am so famous
back in Pakistan that
I get invited on their
celebrity shows.

CELEBRITY MASTERMIND

MY SPECIALIST SUBJECT – IMMIGRATION

CELEBRITY MASTERCHEF

My winning dish →

I'M A CELEBRITY GET ME OUT OF HERE

In Pakistani version they send us to India and make us eat cauliflower curry – disgusting

BIG BROTHER

All the men here are my brothers →

Being a community leader in Sparkhill and a celebrity here and in Pakistan has inevitably meant that I've started to rub shoulders with increasingly famous people:

From Birmingham's previously most famous son, Jasper Carrott.

To queen of daytime TV Lorraine Kelly!

. . . To queen of the whole bloomin' country!

Handy Guide to Dealing with Fame

It's very important, once you reach the height of fame, to behave in a manner appropriate to your position. So here are my top tips:

1. Get a good agent, but be aware they take 10 per cent. So maybe get a good Asian, they only charge 5 per cent.

2. It's not easy being a celebrity. There's a lot of pressure that people don't think about. You always have to be at your best – clean and tidy. I always make sure that I have a bath at least every week and wear clean underwear most days.

3. People will always want a piece of you, particularly Mrs Bilal – if you are reading this, Mrs Bilal, you shouldn't be. Remember, there's an injunction.

4. Because you are in the public eye, you are often asked to open things – like supermarkets, if your stupid wife is on the early shift and forgets her key.

5. It's always important not to lose the common touch. I am proud that I never take advantage of people's good nature. This is why I always sign autographs and never charge more than five pounds for them. Unless they're Indian. Ten pounds or no deal.

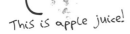

This is apple juice!

6. The other big bonus to being famous celebrity is the freebies! People want you to promote their things. You need to be respectful of such people because these idiots will pay money to put your face on their product. I am getting something called a vajazzle on Monday – I can't wait. Alia is very jealous and surprised. I think it might be a car – a Volkswagon Vajazzle.

7 The other day, I got my own escort at Buckingham Palace – escorted straight off the premises, how rude. How was I to know you need an invitation to a garden party? I just told them I knew Liz and she had invited me, gave them a bottle of Fanta and strolled in.

8. Never drink too much at an awards bash. I drank so much apple juice once at the BAFTAs that during David Attenborough's acceptance speech I nearly wet myself.

9. Always be well presented when on the red carpet. The other day though, I really got the red carpet treatment. That was at Carpet World. I was a bit annoyed because they wouldn't let me swap it for laminate flooring, which is much easier to clean.

10. Image is vitally important. So always take your nose clippers with you (I learned that from Gloria Hunniford).

11. Always respond to fan mail (I get my daughter to do it).

12. Be wary of bad PR, or Pakistani Relations. I had to disown my cousin Ahmed after he was caught with his pants down on Hampstead Heath.

237

Getting Our Country Back

For the final section of this book I want to congratulate the Great British public on the referendum vote earlier this year. Finally, we got our country back. Well bloomin' done! Let me explain . . .

If you look back at British history it's quite clear to see what's important to our brilliant country. Let me illustrate this by showing you three Great Britons.

First of all, who is this?

1.

It's the **Duke of Wellingtons!**
Famous for these:

His parents loved him so much they named him after the local pub.

2.

Here we have
William The Conquerers,
famous for being
champion at conkers.

And finally:

3. Lulu

I love Lulu. In fact I love saying it. You know why? In our Pakistani Punjabi language a lulu is also the word given to a man's down belows. And let me tell you, back in the seventies my lulu made me want to shout as well.

So there are three Great Britons. What connects them all? No, they're not all ginger. No, they haven't all competed in Eurovision Song Contest. Let me help you. Duke of Wellies, where is he from? The Ireland, that's right. Willy Conkers? Yes, he is from the French, and finally we have Lulu, who is from the Scotland. So, what is the one thing that connects these three people when we talk about 'Getting Our Country Back'. The one thing we must never forget? And if we failed to cherish it, many people like this would never have been Great Britons. What is it? I'll tell you - Immigration. They're all immigrants!

So yes, we do need to GET OUR COUNTRY BACK. Back to where it was when we Pakistanis arrived. When we were the last lot of the immigrants and we didn't have any of these Poles here! I agree there are too many Eastern Europeans coming to this country, taking our jobs, jobs meant for us Pakistanis!

We should be proud because, let's face it, immigration is Britain's greatest invention! If you don't believe me just take a look at some of the others:

English food

English people make the worst food. Yorkshire puddings? I tried it with custard and ice cream and it's flipping disgusting. It's not a flipping pudding! It tastes like crispy air and goes all soggy. Give me custard creamies any day.

Camping

What is it with English people and their desire to sleep in a field? 'Getting back to nature'? If you want to sleep next to animals, go and stay with my uncle in Pakistan. Apparently now you can pay silly money to stay in a yurt! Pakistanis have been moving over here for forty years trying to get away from living in yurts.

Speed Bumps

What a silly invention these are. They have the opposite effect than the one intended. You can't speed on them at all! You have to drive really slowly or you bump the underside of your car. What an utterly selfish thing to put in the road.

Sinclair C5 car

This isn't a car, it's a toy! Be careful if you buy one of these online because they are much smaller than you think. It's a real struggle to get me, Mrs Khan and the family in when we go to the mosque, and it doesn't go very fast at all once everyone is crammed in.

If you look closely at this picture, you can see the defect. The guy who designed it is a bloomin' ginger!

Trainspotting

Now I really don't understand this game. You go to the train station and look at a train and write the number down. I tried to play this in Pakistan but it was no good – there was only one train and you couldn't see the number because of all the people clinging on the side.

So, immigration is good but we can't just let everyone in. We have to make sure it's a certain type. You know, keep the good ones coming (Pakistani) and keep out the riff raff (Indians and everyone else). How do we do that? Well, this country has something called the citizenship test. But I've looked at it and it's no good. So I've put together my own version:

THE CITIZENKHANSHIP TEST

1. As you intend to come to Britain. What country is the best in the world?

A. PAKISTAN

B. BRITAIN

C. INDIA

2. Who is the best cricketer in the world?

A. IMRAN KHAN

B. MOEEN ALI

C. SACHIN TENDULKAR

3. What is the best food in the world?

A. PAKISTANI CURRY

B. CUSTARD CREAMIES

C. VEGETABLES

4. Who would you vote for in the local elections?

A. A Pakistani

B. Conservative, Labour or the other one

C. A foreigner

5. If you are womans who will you vote for?

A. I will ask my husband

B. I don't know

C. I will make up my own mind

6. If I get a job as a traffic warden and I see Mr Khan parked on double yellow, I will . . .

A. Get a selfie with him

B. Probably let him off

C. Fill out the paperwork

7. When greeting someone in the street I will say . . .

A. Asalaam Alaikum. I love Muslims

B. All right, mate?

C. Something foreign

8. When seeing a woman in the streets of the UK, I will . . .

A. Stare at them incessantly

B. Wolf whistle

C. Run after them

9. When asked for directions in the street, I will . . .

A. Point them towards the local mosque

B. Point them towards the local pub

C. Wobble my head a lot

10. When living in Britain, the thing I promise to do most is . . .

A. Wear my Pakistani cricket top

B. Shop at my local Pakistani shop

C. Brush my teeth with mouthwash

Thank you for taking my test. Now it's time to find out if you need to
pack your bags . . .

IF YOU ANSWERED MAINLY 'C's

I'm afraid you are not what we are looking for. We need to keep Britain British (and Pakistani). Too much foreign things causes us problems. Also if you are Indian you are far too small and we won't be able to see you driving your cars or crossing the road. Please make your way back to India. I hope they'll have you back. You'll be lucky as Indians rarely take anything back. Just try Desai Cash & Carry on Stratford Road.

IF YOU ANSWERED MAINLY 'B's

Whilst not ideal you are allowed to stay, but I must see improvement. I suggest growing a beard, visiting the local mosque and more importantly doing some research into British life. I recommend purchasing the *Citizen Khan* DVD for assistance. You'll soon be up to scratch.

IF YOU ANSWERED MAINLY 'A's

Asalaam Alaikum, brother. Welcome to your new home. Please make yourself at home and follow your Community Leader, Mr Khan. Just a reminder: as a Muslim don't do anything without consulting Mr Khan and allow him to talk on your behalf. Please begin by following me on the twitter (@therealmrkhan) and buying my *Citizen Khan* DVD.

BRITPAKISTANIA RULES

If you failed the test, why you reading this? Get on the plane!

If you didn't – congratulations! You've passed the test, so you're on your way to this wonderful country. Just bear in mind there are a few things you'll need to know:

1. If you're out in town on a Saturday night and a white person comes up to you talking gibberish, don't assume they're Eastern European. They're just drunk!

In fact, it's probably best to avoid going out into town on a Saturday night generally. Or if you live in Doncaster it's best to avoid going out into town on a Sunday, Monday, Tuesday, Wednesday, Thursday, or Friday as well.

2. Don't be fooled by this red box

Open the door and you'll soon realise that it is, in fact, a public lavatory.

3. What to wear is very important. In Britain you must remember to dress suitably for each occasion throughout the year. Here's an example:

Jan	Feb	Mar	Apr
May	Jun	Jul	Aug
Sep	Oct	Nov	Dec

4. Queuing.

This is very important. You'll need to somehow unlearn this:

And get your head around this instead:

5. Britain prides itself as being the fashion capital of the world, so you'll need to invest in some of these.

Getting Our Country Back: The new PM

So I'm glad we got our country back. We must thank UKIP for this. Probably the biggest, most important party in this country today. No, not that one. I'm talking about the other one. My UKIP stands for U Know I'm Pakistani! You'll thank us one day . . .

Don't forget, when it comes to running the country I'm the only PM you need – A Pakistani Muslim!

Acknowledgements

I would like to thank the wife Mrs Khan for letting me order pizza and not eat her cooking whilst writing this book. I would like to thank my daughter Alia for letting me use her laptop (I can't believe all the FaceTime wrong numbers you get from all these young men). Also thank you to other daughter. Many thanks to all the people at the BBC for allowing me to broadcast my documentary on the TV, without which there would be no book, no new garden furniture and no money to send Naani back to Pakistan.

If you would like to keep in contact you can find me on the Facebook, follow me on the twitter (@therealmrkhan) and you can meet me at Nandos Star City Birmingham most Fridays after prayers. Other places you are guaranteed to meet me are Mr Ali's Cash and Carry most Sundays. I am normally there for five hours as that is how long it takes to fill the car with toilet roll. You can also find me on the first day of every Next sale.

Finally, as a Muslim it's important that I pay respect and gratitude to the great one. Without him, we would not be here today. Imran Khan, the greatest cricketer of all time and my cousin. Thank you.

See you soon sweetie darlings,

mr. khan.

Image credits

BBC
Pages 5, 6–7, 100, 104, 111, 116, 166, 172, 174–175, 182, 204 top , 206–207, 212–213

iStock
Pages 2 map, 5, 6 frame, 11 bottom, 12–13, 14, 15, 18 top, 19, 20, 22, 24, 25, 27, 35, 38, 39, 40, 41 top & middle, 42–43, 44–45, 46–47, 54, 56, 65, 70–71, 72, 73, 74, 77, 80, 88, 91, 92, 96, 101, 104, 110, 114–115, 118–119, 120–121,128–129, 130–131, 132–135, 136,138–139, 140, 142–143 background, 144, 148–149, 150, 152, 153, 154, 158–159, 162 prayer mat, 164, 173 top, 176, 180, 183, 187, 190, 198–199, 200–201, 202, 205, 208, 216, 219, 220, 221, 222, 224, 225, 226, 227, 233, 235 bottom, 237, 240, 241, 242, 243, 249, 251, 252

Shutterstock
Pages 12–13, 16, 19, 28, 29 top, 30, 41 bottom, 54 middle, 55, 57, 58, 67, 82–83, 97, 118–119, 188, 120–121, 122–123, 151 base, 168, 173 flag, 177, 178 tinsel, 185 tinsel, 205, 221, 237,249

Getty Images
Page 64 top Humphrey Spender/Stringer/Getty Images
Page 64 bottom Loop Images/Getty Images
Page 80 Daniel Munoz/Stringer/Getty Images
Page 81 Popperfoto/Getty Images
Page 85 top David Munden/Popperfoto/Getty Images
Page 85 middle Alexis Cuarezma/Stringer/Getty Images
Page 85 bottom Gregg Felsen/Getty Images
Pages 86–87 Nicolas Asfouri/Getty Images
Page 92 left Sarah Ansell/Getty Images
Page 92 right Bob Thomas/Popperfoto/Getty Images
Page 108 Luca Teuchmann/Getty Images
Page 163 DEA Picture Library/Getty Images
Page 189 Imran Khan The AGE/Getty Images
Page 211 NurPhoto/Getty Iamges
Page 233 bottom Corbis/Getty Images
Page 243 David Levenson/Getty Images
Pages 245–246 NurPhoto/Getty Images

ALAMY
Page 10 bottom Tim Graham/Alamy Stock Photo
Page 11 imageBROKER/Alamy Stock Photo
Page 18 bottom Denise Felkin/Alamy Stock Photo
Page 21 Chronicle/Alamy Stock Photo
Page 26 bottom Coconut Aviation/Alamy Stock Photo
Page 29 middle Trinity Mirror/Mirrorpix/Alamy Stock Photo
Page 29 bottom Peter D Noyce/Alamy Stock Photo
Page 48 top Paul Doyle/Alamy Stock Photo
Page 66 A.P.S. (UK)/Alamy Stock Photo
Page 67 top WFPA/Alamy Stock Photo
Page 68 top ravelib prime/Alamy Stock Photo
Page 68 bottom Steve Davey Photography/Alamy Stock Photo
Page 69 David Reed Archive/Alamy Stock Photo
Page 72 Tom Craig/Alamy Stock Photo
Page 90 epa european pressphoto agency b.v./Alamy Stock Photo
Page 94 Jonathan Larsen/Diadem Images/Alamy Stock Photo
Page 96 London Aerial Photo Library/Alamy Stock Photo
Page 103 Pictorial Press Ltd/Alamy Stock Press
Page 105 INTERFOTO/Alamy Stock Press
Page 112–113 LH Images/Alamy Stock Photo
Page 126 dbimages/Alamy Stock Photo
Page 135 Alex Segre/Alamy Stock Photo
Page 148 bottom S&G/S&G and Barratts/EMPICS Sport
Page 181 Michael Burrell/Alamy Stock Photo
Page 183 Curry pot Ruby/Alamy Stock Photo
Page 191 picturesbyrob/Alamy Stock Photo
Page 204 bottom Midland Aerial Pictures/Alamy Stock Photo
Page 216 bottom Midland Aerial Pictures/Alamy Stock Photo
Page 218 Joseph Clemson/Alamy Stock Photo
Page 223 Brenda Kean/Alamy Stock Photo
Page 230–231 Blend Images/Alamy Stock Photo
Page 232 chair Four sided triangle/Alamy Stock Photo
Page 241 Pictorial Press Ltd/Alamy Stock Photo
Page 242 Andrew Aitchison/Alamy Stock Photo

Rex Features
Page 67 middle ITV/REX/Shutterstock
Page 108 top Andrew Parsons/REX/Shutterstock
Page 118 Ken McKay/ITV/REX/Shuttersock
Page 235 Ken McKay/ITV/REX/Shutterstock

Page 106 and 107 Al Ashford

All other photos by James Eckersley